Career Success in High Tech

by

Brian Larson

Career Success in High Tech

by

Brian Larson

Copyright © 2014 by Brian Larson.

All rights reserved. No part of this publication can be reproduced or transmitted in any form or by any means, without permission in writing from the author.

ISBN-13: 978-1497338265
ISBN-10: 1497338263
BISAC: BUS037020: BUSINESS & ECONOMICS / Careers / Job Hunting

About the Author

Brian Larson is a systems specialist in factory automation, a college professor and an author. In the last two decades he has worked for more than seventy-five companies in nine countries abroad and the majority of our fifty United States. He has helped the Russians refine aluminum in the vast forests surrounding St. Petersburg, developed real-time control networks for several fortune-500 companies and worked in top-secret facilities for the U.S. Government at Los Alamos National Laboratory, designing nuclear weapons dismantlement systems.

Brian Larson holds a Bachelor of Science and a Master of Science, both in Computer Science. He has worked inside and outside the office-cubical life as the Vice President of Development for a software company, a lone-wolf telecommuter and an Internet entrepreneur. He has hired, fired, trained and advised hundreds of individuals.

As an author, Brian is a member of SFWA (Science Fiction and Fantasy Writers of America) and has won awards for his numerous science fiction novels (written under the penname B. V. Larson). Other books bearing his name include the textbook series *Computers: Understanding Technology* published by EMC Paradigm (co-author: Floyd Fuller).

Brian resides in California with his wife Alma (a network administrator) and their three children Benjamin, Amanda and Keith.

TABLE OF CONTENTS

Introduction

Part I : Breaking into a Technical Career
    1   Chaos Breeds Opportunity
    2   The College Degree Excuse
    3   The Self-Confidence to Leave School
    4   Types of Jobs and What You'll Really Do

Part II : Getting the Right Job
    5   Job-Hunting
    6   Using the Internet
    7   The Hiring Process
    8   Fast-tracks and Backwaters
    9   How Close Are You to the Money?
    10 Management Cultures
    11 Family Kingdoms
    12 Self-Employment
    13 Job-Hopping

Part III : Keeping Your Job and Moving Up
    14 Surviving Your New Job
    15 The Work Bitching Circle
    16 Stress-Management
    17 How NOT to Make Enemies
    18 Travel, Opportunity and Your Family
    19 How to Manage Techies
    20 Take-Overs and Lay-offs
    21 Resigning, Going Broke and Getting Fired

Introduction

"Necessity is the mother of taking chances."

--- Mark Twain

Are you looking for a new career? Are you just out of high school, the military, college—or are you about to be laid off? Are you bored with your job and looking for something new, something better? Then this book is written for you.

Everyone reaches critical decision-making points in their lives. Studies show Americans now switch careers an average of seven times during their lives.

Seven times, they will make a fateful choice about how they will spend the majority of their waking hours. If it's your turn this year, if your number has finally come up, then this book is for you.

Why? Because this book examines technical careers. That covers a lot of ground. Recent studies by the University of California indicate that over half of the new jobs created nationwide at the turn of the century were classified as technical jobs. This huge slice of the employment pie will continue to grow dramatically.

New jobs are where the opportunities exist for those without experience. New techie jobs aren't the first on the chopping block when management mouths evil words like "down-sizing and cost-cutting". On that grim day, it is those who stand in the way of technology who fall first.

I'm sure you've already brushed up against technology. Maybe you don't like it. Maybe it scares and intrigues you at the same time. Maybe an ATM ate your bankcard. Or maybe a machine eliminated your last job.

We live in a gizmo-driven world of digital wonders. Most of us come to at least *consider* a technical career. How could we not consider it? The richest man on the planet runs a software company. Ads for tablets and cellular phones bombard our senses. Medical discoveries are on the news nightly. Nanites and robots are just around the corner. Technology screams in our faces, and we now take it for granted that our children will mature into a radically different world.

Whether technology in the workplace thrills, frightens or annoys you, it's time that you knew more about it.

Part I - Breaking into Technical Careers

This section explains what technical jobs are all about. It will help you decide if a technical career is for you. Don't be one of the thousands that train for years for something they don't enjoy.

Part II - Getting the Right Job

Part II will help you find the right technical job. It will lead you through the job-hunt, the interview process and finding the right company. You'll also learn how to size up a company offering you a job, and how to interview *them*.

Part III - Keeping Your Job and Moving Up

Once you have the right job, you need to keep it. Part III will help you keep what you've gained and move your career forward. It focuses on how to snatch up the next opportunity to advance and teaches you how to build your skills so you will be ready to jump when the time comes.

PART I: BREAKING INTO A TECHNICAL CAREER

Chapter One
Chaos Breeds Opportunity

"If at first you do succeed—try to hide your astonishment."

--- Los Angeles Times Syndicate

What are technical jobs like? Why are there so many technical jobs? What kind of technical jobs are out there? Which one is right for me? How much training do I need to get started?

All of these questions will be answered in the following chapters. First, let's study the nature of technical work and clarify how it differs from other types of work.

The Nature of Technical Work

One of the first responses I get from people entering into the technical world comes in the form of a complaint. The complaint goes something like this:

> *This stuff is messy. I can't seem to finish anything easily and cleanly. I really miss working the phones and punching in numbers on my old keyboard.*

The first thing I do is agree with them. Technical work isn't clean. Everything is harder than it should be. Everything takes more time and money than the salesman said it would. Just getting your home computer hooked to the Internet can be a trial.

The second thing I do is explain that this characteristic is the very reason why high-paying jobs abound in technical work. To illustrate my point I give them a hypothetical situation:

Imagine that the tax system changed. Imagine that every company in the land had a unique set of tax laws to follow. Different rates, different deductions, different due dates, etc. If this happened, the tax accountants would be up in arms. They would claim that the system was absurd, and that only confusion and chaos would come of it. And they would be absolutely right.

But, consider this: wouldn't tax accountants, the good ones, become harder to find? And if they were harder to find, wouldn't they tend to make more money? Anything that is rare costs more as the competition for it drives the price up. Since the job would be more difficult, and skilled people would be rare and sought after, there would be plenty of jobs around.

Just as important, since it would take a while for a new accountant to learn the ropes at each new job, the existing staff would become harder to replace. So the individual accountant would be more valuable because of his or her specialized knowledge.

This is exactly the situation with technical jobs. The long learning curve, the lack of standardization—the sheer chaos of modern technology is what makes it worth money. I must remind at least one engineer or technician a week that they owe a lot to the mess they have to deal with every day. I get many opportunities to do so because technical people are always complaining of the nightmare of details and changes they must deal with regularly.

I like to remind them too, that if everything were calm, normal and worked right on the first try, they wouldn't have a job at all. This seems to ease some of their pain at times. If you're in the same boat, or training yourself to be, listen to this:

> ***We are getting paid to fix things. We are getting paid to make things work. If things were easy to fix, or if they worked right away, we wouldn't be necessary.***

Therefore, we should see every piece of malfunctioning hardware, every program with a bug in it and every angry, ignorant customer as an opportunity.

I worked for a software company in the nineties as V.P. of Engineering. One day I went with the company president to talk to the technical support staff. Their spirits were sagging. We had just released a software update to all of our customers that had major flaws. The phones were ringing off the hook and all of the support people were under heavy assault. This is what the president told them:

"I know it's hard to listen to endless complaints, but at least you are all busy. Before, I was considering a lay-off in this department, but now I'm happy to say that we can't afford to lose a single one of you."

Needless to say, the technical support people weren't thrilled with this news, but it did sink in. Their jobs depended on problems. In a perfect world they would be on the unemployment line.

This same premise is no less valid now. When I first heard that the Internet was going to go commercial, I foresaw nothing but a giant hairball of technical problems. Could they get the phone lines to carry high-speed data? Could the supercomputers and the wires that connected them carry the new load? Who was going to provide the services that would attract the customers and keep them?

That giant hairball came to rest directly upon the shoulders of the technical work force. And it was a blessing! Billions of hours of labor have already gone into the thing, and countless billions more will follow. Careers have appeared where none were before.

The very curse of the Internet is its true magic in disguise. Let's face it, the thing still doesn't work as cleanly as TV. But it works well enough to get everyone to want it—enough to make them wish to make it work better. There lies the magic: an explosion of money, jobs and careers.

The lesson is that chaos does breed opportunity. Every technical nightmare, every design flaw in the system, every bug in the software is truly gold. The kind of gold that we technical types get to take home and spend.

But there is a second lesson here. Something that follows from the idea that chaos makes work:

> *If we, the technical work force, get paid to make things work, then we must continually find new things to fix. That means that we will never be done with learning.*

And indeed, this is the case. Much of the technical work force tends to follow the newest technology like herds of caribou, grazing until an area is barren and then moving on.

In fact, it is the most nomadic types that do the best. For more on this topic, see the chapter on Job-Hopping. It is perfectly natural not to want to be a nomad, however. It is possible to find a nice niche and remain in it for years. Until recently, people could stay in a technical niche for their entire lives. Today, however, this is no longer a realistic expectation for anyone who isn't close to retirement.

Every year, technology changes the world. Every year it changes it more, and faster, than it did the year before. The rate of change is accelerating, not slowing down, and it has been doing so for several hundred years. This means that we, the herd of caribou, can't afford to stay in one place too long. It is as if summer and winter were closer together each year, and we, the helpless nomads, are left chasing the sun and the good green grass forever.

The learning curve is never-ending. A thousand times I've heard complaints from people who finally master something technical only to find that the rule had already changed by the time they went to apply it. This can be frustrating, but we should remember that if things didn't change, many of us would eventually be out of work. Instead of being annoyed by change, I encourage people to embrace change as a source of security. Each new challenge represents an opportunity. Each new field of grass means that the herd will eat again, at least for another season.

The final point of this chapter is now upon us:

Since change breeds opportunity, and change requires continual learning, then those who stop learning are in trouble.

Our nature for the last several thousand years has been to settle in one place and make a safe, comfortable home of it. We even like the idea of guiding our kids into the same niche, hoping that they might enjoy it as much as we have.

In the technical fields, getting too comfortable is a danger. Every technological niche eventually fades, just as every field of green grass is eventually grazed down to stubble. If you don't believe me, just ask your local slide rule sales representative. Or consult the ghosts running the typewriter service center. Remember Whiteout? Cassette tapes? Onionskin typing paper for "easy erasure"? Some of you might still have this stuff, but I don't. The time for those products has come and gone.

It is very easy, especially as our youngest days pass, to settle into a niche and try to stay there. Humans are excellent at rationalization. We are very skilled at it. To keep ourselves from having to work on learning anything new, we will apply our rationalizations. If you hear yourself saying any of the following, start to worry:

> *Sure, there aren't as many new jobs in (fill-in your comfortable niche here) anymore, but I'm still making a good living.*

... or ...

> *We have a lot of loyal customers in our information service area. They don't want to*

> *learn anything new. Online shopping trends aren't really a threat.*

... or worse yet ...

> *It's an old system, I'll admit that. They don't even sell it anymore. But everybody in this business has one, and it would cost them too much to buy one of the new systems.*

... or even worse ...

> *I'm not worried. There's no way they'll ever put this industry up on the web.*

If you've recently said anything like one of the above statements, you're in denial. If these statements bother you, and you're frowning right now, *you're in serious trouble.* If you are feeling defensive about your niche, that's a sure sign that the time to move on is *right now*. Probably, many people have already fled to new areas.

Technology is a double-edged sword. It offers fantastic opportunities for new people to rise, but it can quickly chop you down to size, too. Think about what you would do if you were laid off tomorrow...

Let's say at three in the afternoon.

They like to do it on Fridays. That way, if you get seriously angry you've got no one to yell at for a few days—and by then your anger will have run out and you will have probably sunken into a blue funk.

It has happened to me and I've done it to others. It happens to a lot of people. Don't let it happen to you. Or at least, if it does, be as prepared as you can be.

Chapter Two
The College Degree Excuse

"Perseverance is not a long race; it is many short races one after another."

--- Walter Elliott

The best programmer in the Information Systems Department was Beth. She could do everything, she knew everything and she'd been there the longest. If a machine broke, she could fix it. If the install procedure on the disk didn't work, she could rewrite it and have it working before the software company's technical support staff bothered to call us back. She was the best, and everyone knew it.

Then one day she came to me, as I was her supervisor, to tell me she had made a disastrous discovery. The accounting department had handed her a flash drive to run a report. The drive they'd carelessly given her had the company payroll figures on it. Unable to restrain her natural curiosity, she now knew what everyone in the company was paid. She'd also found out that she made less than practically everyone in the department. Even some of the secretaries were edging her out.

Why? She had to ask and I should have told her right then, but I decided to go to the president and discuss it directly with him, first. Was it because of her performance? No, she was the best, and everyone knew it, including her. Was it because she was female? No, she had already figured that out by the time she came to me. Most of the department was female, and they were all making more than she was.

I did go to the president, making a case that we might lose her if we didn't act fast. Naturally, I didn't mention the payroll spreadsheets. That wouldn't have made anyone happy. I simply said that she knew she was underpaid and wasn't pleased. Unfortunately, while I was negotiating for her, she went to another member of management and pleaded her case. There, she got the blunt answer:

"Well Beth...you know...you don't even have a degree."

And there she had it. Performance had nothing to do with it. She was missing a college degree. She had reached the paycheck threshold where those in power balked and refused to pay more. At least, not to someone who hadn't gone through the same higher education system that they had. She wasn't "An Officer and a Gentleman". She was an enlisted recruit, part of a different class.

This sort of shortsightedness occurs more often in less technically advanced companies, but it's common at some level everywhere. Sure, there are plenty of reasons why a college degree is a valid measurement of someone's skill, responsibility and commitment. But there are plenty of ineffective employees who have degrees. Because of these realities, I believe the tendency to underpay people without degrees stems from the people in power themselves.

Many people don't like to think that their underlings are smarter than they are. This becomes a particular problem in the area of technology. Technology makes them feel stupid. Everyone who is unfamiliar with a computer goes through a period of looking like a fool before they master it. This is difficult to take for upper-management types, who've often made a career of never looking foolish. It's easier for them to take this feeling of foolishness if the people who handle the technology at least have college degrees. They can say to themselves:

"This fellow has worked long and hard like a monk on a mountain to learn this skill. It's not that the fellow is smarter than I am, it's the training."

They can also retain some dignity by considering that they went through the same process, but with a different educational goal. They can feel superior in their own field.

It is much more difficult, however, for them to face people who just seem to know everything by picking it up on the job. If this is possible, then why haven't they done it? The conclusion they tend to reach is that they must not be too bright. Never mind that they put all their efforts into skills that the technical person probably doesn't have. All they can see is someone with no apparent special training doing things they couldn't begin to understand.

There is another reason for discrimination against technical people without a formal education. The reason is simple ignorance. Often, management is so disconnected from the technical world that they can't judge the difficulty of one technical feat vs. another. This means that they simply don't know how good someone is. All they have to go on is experience and education.

The degree, then, becomes an excuse to pay you more. It is evidence of your ability that management can understand and clearly measure. They empathize with college grads because they went to school, too.

Technical schools that offer certificate programs help, but often aren't enough to appease management. After all, in most cases your manager went to college. That means they don't know what you really did at Network Tech. Certificates help more if you already have a degree.

An Associates (two-year) degree helps too, but isn't enough to completely break the barrier with management. In most cases it is the Bachelors Degree that will give you the best return on the investment. People with degrees are officers. They are in a different class. At least, that seems to be the opinion of many in management.

A Masters Degree can be an excuse to pay you even more, but it is not the significant leap that the Bachelors Degree gives you. Unfortunately, in a career sense a Doctorate is often counterproductive. By this I mean it tends to narrow, rather than broaden, the number of jobs for which one can apply. People tend to be afraid of someone called a "doctor". They often tend to think of them as residing only in universities, like exotic zoo animals.

Now back to Beth, who had just learned that she was cashing the smallest paycheck in the department. In Beth's case, I was unable to get for her anything more than a pat-on-the-head type of raise. She soon quit the company, went to college, and got an excellent job at another firm. By now, she probably makes twice what I do.

There is an important lesson here. Beth wasn't an isolated instance. At least a dozen times I've worked with very competent technical people who reach career roadblocks because they skipped the side-trip through college. I've heard every reason:

I took a few classes, but I found that already knew everything!

My answer to this is: then get an easy A and take credit for what you already know. College isn't just for learning; it is a way for society to *confirm* what you know. If management can confirm it, they will be more likely to compensate you for it.

I have a lot of units, I just find the general education stuff too boring to finish.

Finish it. A sixty-unit Associates degree is worth much more to your checking account than a hundred and fifty units of scattered classes that don't add up to a degree. Without a degree, you'll always be someone who "has taken some units." Employers highly value completion, and take it as a sign that you will complete projects in your career as well.

I simply don't have the time or the money for college.

This is the hardest one to answer. You must measure the sacrifice that college represents against the goals you hope to achieve later. Before you answer this, investigate. Go to the school and talk to people. Find out what they can do for you. After going to the school, talk to your employer and your family. You may be surprised at the support you find.

Oddly enough, Beth's story of being the best talent in the company and not having gone to college is very common. Very often, the best talents don't go to school right away. This is because of the great black hole that technical work represents. Because it is difficult and there is so much demand for it, as soon as someone shows a natural talent for it, they tend to get swept away. Many of my top students are people who got a job right out of high school. After working in the field for some years, they run into the barrier that Beth did, and decide to start college. Often, they're getting easy credit for what they already know.

Another common occurrence is the disappearance of the best students from my college classes. After a year or so of college, the good students get snapped up. Sometimes they get so many job offers in their first year they go for the quick money and never get back on track with school.

Twenty dollars an hour sounds like a fortune to most young people, but after four or five years, it can be inadequate. That's when you need the *college degree excuse*.

Chapter Three

The Self-confidence to Leave School

"Success has a simple formula: do your best, and people may like it."

--- Sam Ewing

The last chapter covered the beneficial points of schooling. There is a darker side, however. Sometimes, for some of us, school becomes too comfortable. It becomes a goal in itself, rather than a means to an end. As I've read at the anonymous joke sites on the Internet:

> *"... and if you stay in college too long, they make you a professor. That means you never get to go home to the real world."*

After some years of training for a technical career, some of us end up liking the training more than the reality of working at a regular job. Worse, people who don't feel a natural talent for their field tend to grow fearful that they "don't know enough". Many people finish their degrees then talk to me about "one more semester". At that point, I get out the want ads and try to bolster their courage.

The fact is that college is never going to teach you everything. You'll be lucky to get 25% of what you need to know from college. That may sound terrifying, but it's true. Attending classes and taking tests and doing projects doesn't compare to eight to ten hours a day of mostly mental labor.

There are no summers off at work. There aren't any vacations at all for most employees until after six months have gone by. You can't cut class and run off to the beach or the pizza parlor, either. At least, not without dire consequences. What will you do for those first six months? You will learn what it is you are really supposed to do. You will learn the other 75%.

Often, what college does for someone is teach them that there is a lot they don't know. This can be frightening. But there comes a time for all of us to leave home, and a time for all of us to leave college.

When? Soon. I firmly believe that everyone in a technical field should get a job in that field, no matter how lowly, at least one year before they graduate. You will learn volumes from even a summer job in your new field. Even if you're just selling stuff at a discount store, or answering technical support questions, or installing equipment on the weekends: DO IT.

The first thing you'll learn is whether or not you like your new field. This isn't always clear for people learning a new skill until they attempt to apply it. If you find you don't like working with hardware, perhaps you would do better with information systems or programming. If you like to be around people more than machines, technical support, sales and technical training are options. Learning early what you like to do can be valuable information. If you know what area of your field you enjoy, you can take courses to better prepare yourself for a job in that specific area.

Second, you'll learn to pay more attention to your education. Not having an answer for your boss and feeling the sweat trickle down your back can do wonders when you take a class and someone utters the answer. Where you might have daydreamed through it before, you will scribble it down and commit it to memory. Now, it means something real to you.

In truth, most employers understand that you aren't going to know everything the first day. If they want that, they shouldn't be hiring someone new. If they want that, they can pay more and get someone else with directly applicable experience.

Most employers know that when they fill a technical position that there is going to be a period of time before the employee comes up to speed. This is because most technical jobs are more detailed and specialized than other types of jobs.

Statements of this nature offend many non-technical people. They see these facts as a sort of arrogance. If a technical job is more difficult than theirs, then that must mean that they aren't as smart, or as hard-working, which isn't necessarily true. No matter how much liberal studies majors would like to deny it, it's true that the technical fields are more difficult. This doesn't mean that technical people are in some way superior as individuals, however. You will get much farther with your career if you avoid any such idea.

Let me explain why the technical jobs are in a different category. For an example let's go back to the example of a tax accountant mentioned in a previous chapter. If you are a tax accountant and you know the U.S. tax code by heart (more power to you) your job is highly skilled, but very focused. The knowledge you have is complex and highly detailed. However, when you examine a new tax return, only the circumstances change, not the *laws* themselves. For tax accountants, the rules change only slightly, in an organized fashion, once a year.

What if you were a tax accountant and when you came to work for a new firm, that firm had an entirely different set of tax laws specifically made for them? What if there were deductions, but they were different, with different amounts and qualifications? What if some of the types of taxes were different, for instance a new tax on water fountain usage, but social security was absent?

In this example, the concepts of having taxes, deductions, tax returns and the like are still there. What are changing are the rules by which these concepts are applied. It would take much longer for a tax accountant to be effective in a new job given this situation.

I must point out that not all technical jobs are like this. If, for example, you are a radiologist, much of what you learned in school will continue to apply wherever you go. The equipment may work differently as the years pass, but for the most part, the changes will be superficial. If, on the other hand, you are a computer support technician, then you can expect continuous shifts and changes in the game. Your knowledge will never be complete. Often, it will seem that it isn't even adequate for the job.

When you get any new job, you have to learn a lot. The company, the people, the work that's expected of you, etc. But in technical work, these are just starters. In addition, you must learn the details of the technical work, and nearly always much of it will be unfamiliar. When the rules *themselves* change, then what you have is a technical job.

Let's take, for instance, the use of databases. Perhaps in school or at your last job you learned how to use Microsoft Access on a PC. So you know databases. But your new employer will probably be using something else, perhaps Oracle, or MySQL. This takes some getting used to. The ideas are the same, but perhaps they are using a different database with a different interface to perform a different task.

You know the concepts, and one specific application. You know 25%.

By now, some of us are probably thoroughly terrified and reconsidering your career choices. Don't panic yet! Not all jobs require such a steep learning curve, and it gets much easier with each year of experience you gain.

If you are a radiologist and the new system uses a database of on-screen images, you'll probably like it after a few weeks. If you are a computer programmer and you know Visual Basic inside out, C++ will be a bit of a shock. But much of what you know is applicable. You just need to learn the new stuff.

Which leads us to the never-ending cycle of learning that any technical field now requires. Which is the very heart of why technical jobs pay well and will continue to pay well into the future. Which leads us to the next chapter.

Chapter Four

Types of Jobs and What You'll *Really* Do

"Whoever says that money can't buy you happiness doesn't know where to shop."

--- *Telegraph Magazine*

Now we have some idea of what a technical job is and why it is different from other fields. But what are the major categories in the technical job market? What is the right entry-level job and where do you want your career to take you from there? This chapter tries to answer these questions.

For specific dollar ranges for salaries, check the appendices at the end of this book. This chapter focuses on the actual work you will perform and the type of person who might do the best in each area. For very current specifics, always check your local magazine rack in the business and technical sections. The market is very fluid and the numbers change monthly. The Internet can also be a valuable source of information on this topic.

1. Equipment Operation

This category includes anything from the position of X-ray technician to data-entry clerk to factory line operator. This is a good entry-level position for anyone and can be a rewarding career for some.

Money:

The amount of money made for equipment operation varies greatly, and is directly linked to the cost, complexity and importance of the machinery being operated. If the equipment is dangerous or requires a special license to operate, the money is better. At present, it can difficult to get beyond the $10 to $12 an hour range, however. Oftentimes the advertised rate is $25 an hour or more, but the catch is that the work isn't full-time, and you are therefore only paid for the length of a rather short contract.

Environment:

Depending on the equipment involved, the environment can be anything from hazardous to mild office surroundings. Due to the nature of the work, however, there are health hazards such as repetitive motion syndrome in any environment.

Stress:

Unless the environment is extreme (toxic, loud, a thousand feet up in a crane cupola, etc.) the stress factor for this type of work is low.

Prestige:

The prestige factor for equipment operators is fairly low. Virtually no one needs to take orders from an equipment operator.

Advancement:

In many organizations, there is a reasonable opportunity for advancement from the position of operator into management. Note, however, that any such advancement would require skills other than the technical ability to operate the equipment. When operators advance, they usually move to another job and stop being operators.

2. Maintaining Equipment

This category includes anyone who installs and maintains hardware, rather than using it themselves. For example, if you were to take a job installing network workstations, or working as an electrician, you would be in this category. Like equipment operation, equipment maintenance is a good entry-level position.

Money:

Like an equipment operator, someone who maintains equipment is tied to the hardware they are working with. The more important and expensive the hardware, the more you will be paid. Equipment maintenance personnel tend to make somewhat more than operators. In other words, someone who installs the computer network or repairs the forklift tends to make more than the computer operator or the forklift driver.

Environment:

Like the operators, the environment depends on the equipment involved. There are usually more health hazards for maintenance people as they may be lifting heavy things, working outdoors, traveling from place to place and working on damaged equipment.

Stress:

There is more stress involved in maintaining equipment than operating it. Keep in mind that if you are an operator, you just run the thing. If it breaks all you have to do is call the maintenance person. If you are the maintenance person, it is your headache to make broken things work—and to keep them working.

Prestige:

Oddly, there seems to be little more prestige for maintenance people than for operators, even though they are generally more skilled. Often, in fact, they have less prestige, possibly because they are dressed for physical work. Somehow, it is hard to be dignified and well-dressed when you are laying cable in a ceiling or crawling around beneath peoples' desks.

Advancement:

Although it is a good place to learn the ropes, in my experience it isn't all that easy to get out of the maintenance department. Part of the problem is that if you are doing good, useful work, there is always more for you to do. Therefore, why should they promote you and then have a hole in their maintenance staff? Of course, if you aren't good at what you do, you aren't going to be up for promotion anyway. In many cases, advancement out of the maintenance department means advancement to another company.

3. Training, Sales and Technical Support

This is the category in which people skills are the most important. If you like to interact with people more than machines, but you still want a technical job for the security it can provide, look into these areas.

Training means educating people. It means giving them the technical knowledge that you have. Technical sales is a great career area for anyone who can do it. Technical support usually means answering e-mail and phone calls from people with technical problems.

Money:

These three areas are widely spaced as far as money goes. Technical support people are usually placed at the bottom. Most people take positions in technical support in hopes of moving up into one of the other areas. Note that this is not true in most nations, where technical support is seen more as a key to customer satisfaction. In the U. S., however, we tend to put our beginners on the front line with the customers.

Training is in the middle of the pay range, but does not have the potential that sales does. In fact, many trainers come from the technical support department.

Sales is at the top—*if you can sell*. No other job on this list can make you more money than sales if you are selling something expensive and selling a lot of it. However, remember this: the product you are selling will oftentimes determine your success as much as your efforts, no matter what the confidence-building gurus say. So, if you're selling bikinis in Alaska, don't expect to buy a new boat with your commissions.

Environment:

All of these jobs come with relatively comfortable office environments. The bottom of the list is often technical support, due to the intrusive nature of the phone and the all-too-often angry person at the other end of it. Sales suffers somewhat from the intrusion of the phone as well.

The other major environmental factor is the travel required for most training or sales jobs. For most people, travel is fun at first, but becomes tiring and disruptive to family life over time. For more on travel, see the chapter on the topic.

Stress:

Stress levels can be fairly high in all three of these categories. Training is probably the least stressful, after you get over your natural stage fright. Technical support and sales tend to be quite stressful. Unlike the trainer, who is just teaching people who want to learn, sales and technical support people are often struggling with others. Salespeople must persuade others to buy, and keep them interested. This can take a lot of energy. Technical support people are the complaint department. They get to hear about, and try to solve, problems that they didn't create. Often this is really an educational process: The caller needs to gently be told that they don't know what they are doing, and that they need to learn a new skill. There can be a lot of stress in telling someone this who doesn't want to listen.

Prestige:

Technical support again gets the bottom rung here. This is partly because most people in this area are new to the company and relatively inexperienced. Next come the trainers, who are respected for their knowledge. Anyone who stands before a group and for hours discusses things that the group doesn't understand tends to earn peoples' respect.

Salespeople get two reactions. Many others in the company dislike them. They tend to think of them as being (as one life-long sales rep and friend of mine used to refer to himself) "highly paid liars". However, management tends to see them in an entirely different light. To management, they are the producers that make dollars, not things to sell. Successful salespeople are cherished by management—but only as long as they are successful.

Advancement:

If technical support has one saving grace, it is that it can be a good place to start. Putting new people in the technical support department gives them a chance to do useful work while learning that 75% they didn't know the first day. It is an employee's chance to thoroughly learn the technical details that make this organization different from all others. Once someone has done well here, they are often allowed a shot at one of the other areas.

Training can be a way into sales or engineering. Often, it is the next step for technical support people who do well. It has the advantage of being doable part time, in conjunction with some other area.

Sales is usually an end in itself. Often, however, people can work their way into management from sales. Whether or not this is true is determined by the ability of the individual and the culture of the organization (again, this will be detailed in a later chapter).

4. Information Systems

This category covers anything from network administrator to systems analyst to Internet webmaster. This is the only category that must involve a computer running a database. Many businesses are now primarily centered around a computer database.

Viewed from the outside, the entire organization of a bank or an insurance company, for example, is dedicated to nothing but maintaining a body of information. Most of the government agencies come under this category as well.

If a bank doesn't know your account balance, or your name, address, etc., what good is it? Everyone who works in such a place is there to feed some detail of information into or out of the database. Without it, the whole organization is smoke.

That's where we, the techies, come in. We are to keep the information flowing. Often fine-tuning it, sometimes overhauling it and always keeping it from getting lost. Information systems people don't just enter data, they control it.

Money:

The money is often good here. This is a field, however, where careful attention should be paid to the nature of the company you are working for. If they don't understand your importance, they won't compensate you properly. Also, this an area in which "the college degree excuse" is critical.

Environment:

Good, if you like an office job. You will rarely breathe unfiltered air or sit under a tree in this occupation. Nor will you suffer from the heat or the cold. Most of the best jobs are in large office buildings in large cities.

Stress:

Middle to high stress is the norm in this field. This is especially true if the organization is new to the technology you are trying to implement. There may also be ignorance on the part of management to overcome.

Prestige:

Good, if the company understands your importance without resenting it. If the company is new to computers, those who have to learn something new will not like you. If computers are commonplace, they will value your talents more.

Advancement:

If the company is heavily based upon the flow of information, there is often a nice career ladder built into the I.S. (information systems) department.

If you wish to someday climb into management, however, first study the culture and history of the company. The door might be locked to I.S. people because the company has never had a person from I.S. become a manager before. In general, advancement for I.S. people is easier in a new company where they don't have strict traditions to follow.

5. Research, Programming and Engineering

This is where techie purists aspire to go. These are often people who don't want to wear ties, nor in some cases, even shoes. Who built the first garage-shop computer companies? Here they are. Where do the mad scientists among us belong? Right here.

At least, that is the opinion of many people on the outside. And there is still some truth to it. We've all met or at least seen on TV the stereotypical geniuses that supposedly inhabit dark dens and eat nothing but delivered pizzas and diet soft drinks.

But these days the hard-core engineering crowd isn't always that kind. The money and the prestige of technical work have attracted a larger pool of people into the field. In truth, anyone with some degree of talent can do this type of work. It has been the desire that has been missing for most of us.

Money:

Again, here the money is good. Often, it is slightly better than I.S. Unlike I.S., people in highly technical fields are fairly well understood. If you work for a manufacturing company, for example, you will find there have been computers in the engineering department for years.

Management better understands engineering people because the computer revolution came to the engineering-based companies long ago. I.S. people are now seen more often as invaders than engineering people. Even engineering people can be viewed with mistrust when they are moving to new ground, however.

Compensation in this area depends greatly on how close you are to the money. See chapter 10 for details.

Environment:

Sadly, there is some truth to the "dark den" talk. For many programmers and engineers, the florescent bulb is their only companion. Unlike most office jobs, the mental demands of this kind of work require long hours of focus. There are meetings, but generally fewer than for other types of office jobs. If you like to concentrate and hate meetings anyway, this might be a positive factor.

Stress:

Middling to High. When deadlines come due, overtime and sweat appear. For most engineering people, however, the job is fairly relaxed. If the projects are long, you can work at your own pace without much stress. If time is short, however, or if there are unforeseen problems, life can be difficult.

Prestige:

Yes, and no. What you oftentimes have here is the prestige of Spock from Star Trek. Laymen might be in awe of you, but that doesn't always make everyone your friend. This can be reversed if you have good people skills. I once had a friend tell me: "Man, for an engineer, you sure act like a regular guy."

Advancement:

This is very dependent upon the culture of the company and type of organization it is. An engineer working at an electrical contracting company, for example, might climb all the way to the top. On the other hand, the same engineer working at a Savings and Loan is never going to leave the department.

PART II : GETTING THE *RIGHT* JOB

Chapter Five
Job-Hunting

"All of us could take a lesson from the weather, it pays no attention to criticism."

--- *North DeKalb Kiwanis Club Beacon*

Almost everyone hates job-hunting. Job-hunting is the act of selling yourself. For most of us, it is the closest brush we experience in our lives with pure capitalism. There's nothing there but you and the world. The world holds your next car, house and meal in its grasp. Somehow, you must go out and get someone to give you these things in trade for your time, knowledge and skills.

For anyone who doesn't like sales, who feels that asking someone for something is bothering them, job-hunting is particularly difficult. Not only are we about to bother people, but also they may well reject us. Rejection with any sale is hard to take, but when the thing you're selling is yourself, it's even harder.

It sometimes helps to realize that you are only asking other people if *you* can help *them*. You are not begging for help. You are offering a trade: your work for their organization's money. If they don't need your help, then you will find someone else who does. Without this process, there would be no new-hires at a company. Jobs get filled every day, thousands of them. The process is never-ending.

Sometimes procrastination sets in at this point. I've seen more procrastinators among supposed job seekers than any other group.

I recall a friend named Anthony who was a master at it. College ended, they gave him his diploma and he walked with his class. That should have been the end of it, but it wasn't. First, he took a summer school class. He wanted an extra skill. He kept working at his parents' business in the meantime, as he had throughout high school and college. He showed no signs of moving on into the big blue world out there. Soon his family members were buying him books like this one—hoping that something would sink in.

The workload became heavy at his parents' business, so he stopped going to the summer school class and took an incomplete. Somehow, the incomplete grade at school for a class he didn't even really need, since he had already graduated, became a reason to avoid serious job-hunting. It wasn't until the Christmas season that someone finally called out of the blue from a major company and offered him an interview. He finally found himself employed. Later, he learned that his dad had gotten a business associate to make the call.

This worked out well enough for Anthony, but not all of us can hope to be so lucky. Jobs don't come up and grab people too often. It happens about as often as fish jump in your boat when you are out on the lake.

How can you tell if you are procrastinating? The classic mode of operation for procrastinators is to build barriers. Anything will do. For Anthony, it was first his summer school, then his summer job. Sometimes, people will fabricate ways to slow down the search, while not actually halting it. Here are some of my favorite lines:

> ***I can't send my resume to anyone else, because the Conglom Company hasn't responded yet.***

If a company is taking a long time to respond to a letter you sent, then try another company. They will often take months to respond. I'm sad to say that I've worked for companies that sometimes failed to respond at all.

My transcripts won't show my degree officially for three months. They won't be able to tell whether or not I've graduated.

If you explain at the interview that your transcripts will take a bit of time to clear, they will understand. Besides, they can always call the school.

They really still need my help in the stockroom of Dead-end and Sons.

This one always gets me. If you've just finished learning a new skill, didn't you always mean to leave your old job anyway? Believe me, if they need you there, they will never be happy to see you go. Not tomorrow, not next month. You're just going to have to break their hearts.

Do it gently, though. Try to give them a week or two of notice. You may need them in the future. It is very common for people to leave a company to find a better job. It is almost as common for them to come back to that same company later and get a different, more skilled job. You can read more about this phenomenon in the Job-Hopping chapter.

Once we are past all procrastination and are ready to proceed, some of us get overly zealous. It can be just as big of a mistake to send out a thousand resumes as to send out one at a time. You should target the companies and positions you want and are qualified for. Do it carefully, so as to not waste their time and yours.

Try several different approaches. Not all jobs are obtained through mailing out resumes. In fact, less than half are gotten that way. Check around with your friends, family and acquaintances that are connected with the business. Managers often hire on the basis of personal recommendations from trusted employees. In technical fields, this seems to be even more common than otherwise. I don't know how many times I've been asked:

> *"Yeah, nice resume. But is he really good?"*

This brings up the topic of resumes. Plenty of books have been written on the topic, so I'll give you only my best pointers here.

I've hired many people and have had the "pleasure" of reading thousands of resumes. I would suggest the following:

1. Less Is More.

Try to keep it down to one page, if possible. Remember that the whole point of the resume is to get you to the interview. You can tell them the rest there. Think of the resume as your ad. Would you rather review a lot of short, impact ads or a lot of lengthy infomercials? Write short, positive statements about your skills, education and experience. Someone who is wading through resumes will be more likely to pick out something clear and simple that they can read quickly.

2. Write A Simple Objective At The Top.

A one-sentence statement of your employment goals can be crucial. This can be a pain for the resume writer as they will have to tailor this line somewhat for different jobs, but it is often worth it. And remember, you don't always have to put in: "with good opportunities for advancement". Everyone wants to advance; you don't really need to say it.

3. Make It Look Good.

Use nice paper. Have a service print your resume up for you if you need to. It does help. Don't make the paper too dark, however, darker paper is harder to read. White or off-white paper is the best.

Selling Yourself

After the want ads are circled in red and the resumes are pumped out the door and every friend and family member knows you are job-hunting, what's next? *You should try to meet the employers personally.* I'm not suggesting that you just show up at someone's office and sell yourself to whoever will listen. This sometimes works, but is more likely to just annoy people and convince them you're a nut. Instead, try things like job-fairs and industry shows.

Ken, a friend of mine, has worked as a free-lance programmer for many years. This means that he must continually get new contracts, as most of them don't last more than a few months. I've asked him about it and studied his methods.

He never uses a resume. He goes to industry shows and makes friends. He doesn't just slap backs and buy drinks, either. He makes friends by showing a genuine interest in whatever the people at the shows are demonstrating to the public. He listens closely and picks up everything he can. He truly *knows* most of the companies in his field and what they are doing.

After learning what the companies are about, he next tries to help them. Once I watched him talk things over with a company that specialized in building gantry robots. Later, after absorbing a lot of information about their product, he brought over someone from another booth that had a use for gantry robots. Having learned what they are about, he even managed to demonstrate and discuss to this new possible customer how the product worked.

In a very short amount of time, he can become indispensable to people. If something doesn't work, he can save the less technical salespeople by fixing it. At some point, more often than not, someone says:

"Ken, you seem like an employee around here. Maybe we should figure out some way to pay you for all this."

At that point, Ken makes his pitch. He usually already knows some problem they are having and he offers his talents as the remedy. Trusted employees then give his name to management and he is in the door.

At this point, Ken is no longer a stranger. He isn't just a faceless resume, or a voice on the phone. There may not have even been an open position, but there was a problem. Now Ken, everyone's friend, is there to fix it. In the end, that's what all technical work is about:

Fixing Problems.

Chapter Six
The Power of the Internet

"The greatest power is often simple patience."

--- E. Joseph Cossman

This chapter won't tell you what button to push on your Internet web-browser. It won't even tell you what a web-browser is, if you don't know. There are plenty of books out there that cover that information. What it will tell you is *why* you need to learn about the Internet and *what* you can get out of it.

No matter what you've heard, the Internet isn't the answer to all your troubles. It is a source of information, and possibly a source of employment. It can help you get a job, and it can be a job in itself. Anyone in a technical field needs to investigate it, at least enough to learn the basics. Internet literacy is easy to achieve and right now is a skill that would help spruce up any resume.

One thing the herd (by "the herd" I mean the technical work force, including you and me) naturally tries to do is distinguish between technical people who are "with it" and those who aren't. One of the easiest ways for them to put you in one of those categories is your Internet connection info. If you can at least put an Internet e-mail address and a social media page on your resume, you'll have the smell of a winner about you.

Almost everyone knows an Internet address when they see it now, even if they don't really know beans about the Internet. They will be impressed and reassured that you know something trendy. They will take this as an indication that you are current in your knowledge and skills. Of course, this may or may not be the case, but they will take it that way.

Besides appearing "with it" you will also *actually be* somewhat more "with it". By this I mean you will be connected to that growing sector of technical jobs that the Internet is creating. Many high-tech companies are now doing the majority of their employment advertisement on the Internet. There are lots of jobs that are publicly announced *only* on the Internet. These positions aren't just computer jobs, either. The number and variety of these jobs grows daily.

Why advertise for employees solely or primarily on the Internet? The first reason is cost. The Internet is accessible from almost anywhere on the globe, and people looking for a particular type of employment can search it. For an advertisement of this type it works far better than a newspaper. What newspaper can boast unlimited advertising space, accessible from anywhere in the world and at a price that is practically free?

There are more incentives for the companies. The fact that the advertisement is on the Internet means that presumably only people with skills on the net will find it. This is, in a sense, a pre-screening function that is built into the system. If they only want "with it" people, why not advertise where only the "with it" people will see the ad?

The last incentive is convenience. Applicants can send their resumes electronically across the Internet. The reply can go back the same way. If the position closes, the ad can be removed in minutes. All this means that until an applicant is chosen, there is no need for anyone to communicate via disruptive phone calls or stacks of paper mail.

What has and is taking place is the growth of a *virtual community*. This is an open community using social media systems, and anyone is free to join it. But it is at the same time closed and hidden from anyone who is unaware of it. What this means is that you can check every newspaper in a city and not see any mention of jobs that are being filled every day on the Internet.

If you are interested in getting connected, here are some suggestions:

1. First You Need A Fairly New Personal Computer With A High Speed Connection.

You should get directly on to the internet with a high speed ISP. If you plan to work on the web a lot, you may want to consider an upgraded, higher speed connection. If you don't have a computer system, you can get one for around $1000.

2. You Need To Learn How To Use The Internet.

Despite the ads, learning to use the net effectively takes a considerable amount of time. If you are a computer novice, take a course in computer literacy first. If you have a few basic computer skills but aren't an expert, I would suggest you take a course on the Internet. A one-unit community college class or a three-day commercial training is probably all you'll need. If you are adept with computers, you can probably get all you'll need from a few how-to books.

3. You Must Get Connected.

This is a process similar to getting cable TV hooked up to your house. Fortunately, it is usually doesn't require that anyone visit your home. In most cases, getting a connection takes only a phone call. Expect to pay about $30 a month for the service.

4. Get Cracking.

Once you have the equipment, the skills and the service, all you need to do is get on the web and search for jobs. I can't give you any good starting Internet addresses here, as they change constantly. By the time this is published, many of them would be out of service or changed.

Chapter Seven
The Hiring Process

"Life is like riding a bicycle; you don't fall off unless you stop pedaling."

--- Claude Pepper

There are three major steps in the hiring process. The first is the job-hunting stage, which is discussed in the previous chapter. Second is the interview. The last step is the negotiation of terms.

Each step is critical. Understanding the hiring process is one of the keys to success for the applicant. It is important that the applicant understands what he or she should do at each step. It is also important that the applicant understands what the company is doing at each step.

Once the company has contacted the applicant and requested an interview, the second step has been reached. In my experience, it is during this transition from the resume to the interview that people often end their chances without realizing what they are doing.

I have been involved in the hiring process hundreds of times. For years, my duties included recruiting new technical people. I always enjoyed the work and viewed it as helping people and the company. *I also knew as a manager that the best way to make sure that I didn't get ineffective employees was to hire them myself.*

Often, a person would have an impeccable resume, but would blow their chances the moment they came into live contact with me. Here are some of the surest ways people found to cross themselves off of my list:

1. Don't Push Too Much.

I greatly dislike people who call up and try to talk me into interviewing them. Remember, it is the company's choice to interview you—don't push. It is okay to ask if a position is still open, or to ask if your application has been received. Anything else will probably end your chances. Calling more than once or talking for a long time is a very bad move. Calls can be made and can work, but they must be done very carefully.

2. Keep In Touch.

If they were unavailable when I called to ask them to come in for an interview. If I left a message and I wasn't called back within the next working day, they were usually dropped. This is because by that time I had already filled out my interview schedule with a list of candidates who did return my call promptly.

3. Don't Play Hard-To-Get.

Some people were too difficult to fit into my interview schedule. Often, I would offer two or three varied times for an interview. If none of them suited the applicant, there was rarely a fourth. In most cases, you will have to miss some work time or school time to come to an interview. Expect to use up at least half a day on an interview, either the morning or the afternoon.

Interview Prep

Let us assume you have managed to get an invitation to an interview. There are still many pitfalls before the interview begins.

1. Get the Details.

Once you have the interview, you must know where you are to go, when you are to be there and whom you are to see. First get the interview scheduled then ask for specific directions to the interview location. If you sense that the caller is too busy to give good directions, thank them and hang up. Then call back and talk to the receptionist. Often, they give better directions anyway because they do it every day.

2. Dress Your Best.

If you should dress formally, then wear a suit. If you aren't sure, then wear a suit. If you can't afford a suit, do what one of my students did, buy one off the rack and then take it back the next day. (If you are in retail you probably hate me for suggesting this, but it is important. Remember, if people get a new job, they will have the money and the guilt to come back to buy something else at your store.)

I can't tell you how many times I've gotten myself caught on this one: How much do I dress up? Of course, the worst time to miss your cue here is when going on an interview trip, but it is important in general to know the dress code before going somewhere. Back when Scott Paper had a big complex for their corporate headquarters outside Philadelphia (they've since been harshly "downsized") I called ahead of my business trip and asked about the dress code. They told me to it was standard office dress, so I loaded up some slacks and pinstriped, off-white, short-sleeve shirts and flew out there.

When I got there, everyone was wearing three-piece suits. Everyone. There wasn't an arm hair in sight, either, because all their utterly white shirts were long-sleeved and cuff-linked. And there were thousands of them; all dressed alike except for me, with my "colorful" short-sleeved shirts. I felt like the California surfer-boy in sandals, let me tell you. Since I was to be working with them for some time, I had to rush out that night and grab a few jackets off the rack. For weeks, I played "musical clothes" swapping around the few ties, shirts and jackets that I had so that it didn't look like I was wearing the same clothes every day, which essentially I was.

The moral of the story is that you need to be sure, so at an interview it is better to be safe than sorry. You aren't going to get away with running to the mall in the middle of it.

3. Be There Five Minutes Early.

If the interview location is in your town, go there and locate it at least half an hour in advance. If it is out of town, go there an hour or more in advance. This is to give you some cushion in case something goes wrong.

Once you find the place, don't hang around the lobby waiting. Go to a coffee shop and sit there, checking your watch, hair and teeth about every thirty seconds. Then, about ten minutes before the interview, make your arrival and tell the receptionist who you are and who you are to see.

Whatever you do, don't be late—not even five minutes late. Excuses don't matter. Just be there on time. (That's why you come half an hour early).

If you are late, you've probably blown the interview. You have demonstrated to your new employers that you don't care about them. You have wasted their time and can't even arrive promptly for the interview.

Being late to the interview indicates to any employer that you will probably be someone who comes in chronically late.

If you are smooth, however, there is some chance of saving yourself. If you are there fifteen minutes late or less, be cool and don't say anything. Make no excuses unless asked. Quite possibly, the person you are to see is running late too and won't even notice. This is your best hope.

If you are more than fifteen minutes late, especially if you know ahead of time that you can't make it, then call and try to reschedule. Have a brief, believable excuse for the delay. Kids and cars make the best excuses. "I got lost" or "I got sick" are the worst, as they show incompetence on your part. If you are lucky, they may let you have a second chance.

No one gets a third.

4. Equipment List.

Take with you ten copies of your resume, a new notepad and a nice-looking pen. Usually you won't need to take any notes, but if you are ready with the notepad it looks like you care. The resumes are good in case someone has lost or forgotten yours.

What to Expect

Next, there is the interview itself. You made it there, you are on time, you look your best and you seem alert. Now it is time for the show.

There are several types of interviews. Try to figure out what you are facing early in the game so that you know what to expect and can respond smoothly.

1. The Informal Interview

This can occur when a friend asks you to come by the office. Then, perhaps, the manager asks you if you are looking for a job. Or it can happen on the spot in a hotel lobby, a sitting area at a trade show, or even on a plane trip. Informal interviews are powerful, and probably the best, if the person you are talking to really has the power to hire you on the spot. If they don't, there is often a more formal interview step later. If they do have the power, there is no easier way to get the job. This is partly because there isn't any competition to worry about.

2. The Formal Tag-Team Interview

In this case you move from office to office, or people come from their offices to see you. One at a time they get a chance to evaluate you. They then will meet later and make their decisions.

This type of interview is usually good for the applicant. First of all, they don't have to be nervous about facing a crowd. Secondly, if the company uses this kind of interview they probably don't have a lot of applicants. That means you have less competition.

There are two major drawbacks with this type of interview. First, it takes a long time for the applicant, usually hours. This can be nerve-racking and eats up much of your day. Second, this sort of thing tends to be more loosely scheduled and taken less seriously by the people involved. If for some reason you never get to see the real decision-maker, you may be in for a second interview or you may be dropped.

3. The Formal Panel Interview

This type of interview can be terrifying, but at least it is quick and decisive. Normally, everyone who needs to be there will be. On the down side, an organized panel often indicates a lot of applicants. This type of interview is the most structured and often the panel will have a written list of "canned" questions they ask everyone. These questions usually follow a predictable course. This can make it easier to prepare your answers.

Government and big companies love this type of interview so you should expect it from them.

Making Friends

How you should behave in any type of interview is more or less the same. What we are really doing at an interview is making friends. But we aren't doing it in the normal way. It is a much more structured situation.

One of the biggest things to worry about first is your composure. It is best to be calm and cool, at least on the outside. Try not to fidget, scratch or laugh too much. Be serious, but have some sense of humor. Young people in particular tend to laugh nervously. The worst thing you can do is be arrogant or flippant. Take everyone who talks to you very seriously, no matter what you think of them. Even if you are going for a V. P. position, don't disregard the opinion of anyone involved. They may have the power to sink you if they wish.

At some point during the interview you will be asked to talk about yourself. You should restrict your remarks down to *how you can do the job for them*. Don't talk too long and don't stray away from the point.

Very importantly, don't be too personal. In most states, there are laws governing what can and can't be asked by an employer. In California and other states, for instance, employers' can't ask your age, marital status, or about past health or financial problems.

This should be seen as an advantage. It allows you to tell them what you wish to. Most employers want to know these things, but can't ask. During your talk, mention the things that you think might be beneficial to your chances. If you are older or younger than you look and don't want them to get the wrong idea, give them a hint as to your age. If you are going through divorce and bankruptcy, *don't tell them*.

Besides the talk, there will be questions. There are whole books written about what kind of questions to expect, and some may seem quite odd. At least, they do to me. If they are too odd, you may want to take that into consideration when deciding whether or not to take a job offer later. If they are to the point, do your best to explain what you can do for them.

Here are some examples of questions people have been asked at interviews. (This is real, but don't get the idea that *I* asked anybody these things.)

What is your favorite color? What is your favorite animal?

Yes, I'm serious. If you get crap like this, what they are trying to do is perform some kind of "personality-profile" mumbo-jumbo. Try telling them you like crimson aardvarks and see if you get the job. Generally, these questions indicate that there is an oddball in upper management somewhere. Either they don't trust their own judgment of character enough to decide what kind of person you are or they are just "whacked-over-the-chips" as we techies like to say. In either case, this line of questioning should be a big negative in your judgment of them, as it indicates this employer is likely to behave bizarrely in the future.

If (ambiguous reference one) were mated with (ambiguous reference two) would you, in your opinion, get an (ambiguous reference three)?

This is the sort of question that you get on canned interviews that they will refuse to clarify much. The secret plan is to get you to reveal what your *real* knowledge is by what you assume the question to be about. For example, if they ask you about "connectivity" and "distributed management" and you talk about the Internet, they will figure you really know about the Internet. If you start talking about writing a new program to fix the problem, they will assume you are really a programmer, etc. The psychobabble behind this is that people tend to take unclear questions and answer them by falling back upon what they know best.

Ambiguous canned questions are mostly an indicator that they are trying to be cagey. (It is also possible that they are simply without a clue and don't understand the terms they are spouting). Again, you probably have a monkey in the deck of managers at this company. Probably someone who enjoys watching others squirm a bit, and likes to feel superior about it. This is a negative, but not as big as the first one.

At some point they normally give *you* a chance to ask questions. You should have two or three intelligent questions ready to ask. Ask about the company and the job you are applying for. During the questions, don't be the first to ask about money. Let them bring it up, if possible.

Sometimes a form of presentation or demonstration by you is part of the interview. Be over-prepared for this. Whatever you do, make it short and as clear as you can to non-technical people. There will usually be a group of techies and non-techies present. In order to impress them both, you have to do a good technical presentation, but also put in a few low-level details that will make the non-techies feel they learned something too. You see, from their point of view, they are sitting there for hours being bored to death by nerd-stuff that they don't understand. So, if you can pull out a prop or a simple diagram of some kind and make part of the presentation a comparison to everyday events, they will love you for it. You will be remembered as the guy "even they learned something from".

The final phase of the hiring process is the negotiation phase. Normally, this isn't done on the same day as the interview, unless it is an informal one. Once they contact you and offer you the job, negotiations have begun. We have reached stage three.

Most companies are very clear about what you will be doing and how much you will be paid. This isn't always the case, however. Sometimes, people show up to work the first day without knowing how much they are getting paid, or when, or on what basis. This is a bad move for both sides, as it builds up tension for the new employee. Once the job is offered, it is more than fair for you to ask these details. Do it immediately, but politely.

Negotiations are a critical time. Often, two or three years' worth of raises can be earned in the space of a few conversations.

The best and the easiest time in the world to get a raise is before you even go to work.

Six Rules of New Job Salary Negotiations

1. Money is Number One.

For almost everyone, the money is more important than the benefits. Don't get lost looking at various insurance plans. If the job comes with full benefits, that's all you need to know.

2. You Don't Always Need To Haggle.

If they offer a figure first and it seems very reasonable, then take it. Sometimes, particularly in government jobs, they can't give you more even if they want to. But then again, rules are meant to be broken…

3. Haggling Techniques.

If they want you to name a number first, they are being a bit tricky. If you really want to make more money than your previous job, I have a very effective move for you to try:

Tell them how much you were making at your last job and that you would like to make 10% more so that the change is worthwhile. The key here is that you don't have to tell them exactly what you were making before. I caution people to be sincere in almost everything, but this is business.

Let's say, for example, that you are hoping for a 25% increase over your old job. That's big and pushy, but maybe that will make the job worth moving for, or help make that long commute bearable. If you tell them you are making $40,000, there's not much hope of them offering you $50,000. But, if you tell them you are making $46,000, $50,000 sounds much more reasonable. At the worst, they can offer to match you at $46,000, and everybody feels like they got a deal.

Think about it this way: they want your skills and knowledge. You are going to give up your time for some amount of money. You know what you will feel comfortable working for, but if the amount is too much more than the amount you are making some place else, they will feel cheated. If you are just asking for 10% more, then they will feel it is reasonable.

This way, everybody's happy. Even if they just agree to match your "old salary", you can take it and call it a raise. Then they have their new employee at a price that is competitive with other companies. You have the salary and job you want. That was the whole point in the first place, wasn't it?

Don't worry about them somehow learning how much you actually made before. Unless you are going to work for the IRS, they won't.

4. Always Deal In Specific Numbers.

Before you go in come up with a figure that is the lowest you'll take, and a figure that you want to try for. Don't ever talk in terms of ranges. If you ask for something between $45,000 and $55,000, you'll get $45,000.

5. What If This Is My First Job?

If this is your first job, plead ignorance and then name a specific number. Make it a bit high. If they are stunned, you can always back off and say that you don't know what to expect. If they jump at the number, you guessed too low.

6. Don't Name Insane Numbers.

Don't hold out for more unless you really won't work for less. Be professional about it. This isn't a used car buying game. You can blow everything by treating it that way.

On a final note, it is important that you check out the company even while they are eyeing you. You will probably spend a third or more of your waking hours for years with these people. Don't go to work for people that you wouldn't want to take with you on a camping trip.

Chapter Eight

Fast Tracks and Backwaters: Finding Your Niche

"If you're going to be able to look back on something and laugh about it, you might as well laugh about it now."

--- Marie Osmond

Every once in a while, I give what I call the pogo-stick lecture. It goes something like this:

Let's say you really like to pogo-stick. You can bounce around longer than any of your friends. Every night, you come home and spend a few hours pounding around the neighborhood. You get better and better as the years go by. Pretty soon, you never fall off, and you decide to go for the world record. You pogo-stick for days straight, eating your meals while bouncing, watching TV while bouncing... everything while bouncing. You win the world record and you know with confidence that you are the best pogo-sticker in the world. That night, you even get thirty seconds of fame on the evening news.

But will you ever earn a dime for your skill? Probably not. In fact, people will probably get tired of you, then think you are odd and finally begin to avoid you. Your family will at first be amused, and then later they will despair.

Why?

Because nobody wants a pogo-sticker. It is not a skill that this world values.

The moral of the story is that *hard work doesn't* **guarantee** *success.* Hard work is almost always necessary, but unless you are working hard on something people want, they will not reward you for it. When all is said and done, it is far better to work hard on something that the world values.

Every year I see people who are working their hearts out at jobs that are doomed. If the job isn't doomed, then it's stagnant, a dead-end where they are learning nothing useful. This is sometimes worse, as it can go on for longer and leave the employee more out of date when they finally need a new job.

These people often work for companies that are too small, badly-managed, financially troubled or technologically outdated. Often they are overworked and underpaid, as the whole company isn't doing well. They stick with it because they like the other people in the company and don't want to let them down. Besides, the job keeps them safe from job-hunting and from having to learn something new.

In technical jobs this is a losing strategy. Technical work is a roller coaster compared to other fields. Companies boom and bust all the time. In the hi-tech fields especially, there is little chance that you will stick with the same company and the same people for more than a decade. In most cases, the show will be over in less than five years at any job. *That means that you will leave at some point, or be booted out. It is only a matter of time.*

If you see any given job as a temporary arrangement, it is best to work for a company that is going places. Or at least, one that suits your needs and will allow you to get another job when this one fades.

Fast-track companies are often small, young, vibrant companies. If you get in early and are important to the company, you might be able to get a piece of the action in the form of stock options. Multi-millionaires are made this way every year.

The Netscape story is one of the most famous recent examples of fortunes being made. In 1996, when the fledgling company made its debut on Wall Street, the stock soared to four times its initial offered value on the first day. It was the best opening day of any stock in the history of the exchange. Every major employee in the company was an instant multi-millionaire. One twenty-four year-old programmer, for example, owned stock options worth fifty-two million by the close of the first day. The CEO was worth over half a billion. All of this occurred less than a year after the company itself was first formed.

Of course, we can't all work for the next Netscape. But we might work for a place that does rather well in a short amount of time and get rewarded for it.

Then again, we might not. Unfortunately, small companies are also more likely to fail. Thousands go out of business every month. When working for them, you are taking the risk of working long hours, night and day. With the long hours come no guarantees. New businesses often fade to nothing by the end of the year.

I've gone down with a few ships myself. Here are some things to look for that can spell success or failure:

1. The Company Has Money.

Somewhere, somehow, the company needs a pot of money to back it. Success is rare in a vacuum. If the owner is rich or has some other form of strong support, the company will be better able to weather the storms of capitalism. Just as important, they will be able to pay you decently while you work for them. That way, even if the place goes bust, at least you got something out of it.

Many companies fail. They might have good managers and have a great service or product, but they need a supply of money in order to compete. You may have heard that it takes money to make money. It's true.

2. The Management Is Competent.

Just as important as the money supply is smart management. When you meet the managers, the ones at the top, try to judge their competence. Much of your career may depend on their decisions. Look out for managers that are involved in lawsuits. Abusive, absentee or sloppy managers are usually doomed.

A key yardstick you should use to evaluate potential managers is how well they understand what you are going to do for them. It is often dangerous to work for people who don't really know what it is that you do.

Technical equipment is a pain. Rarely does something new and different work immediately. Cost overruns, steep learning curves and unending configuration times are normal and just part of the deal. Unfortunately, many managers don't understand or accept this. If you are responsible for "the new system", ignorant management will first blame you for their bad decisions. With luck, you can get them to blame the sales rep. who sold the equipment to them, but you can almost never get them to blame themselves.

I once was involved with a company that sold a piece of software that never actually worked. This didn't keep them from selling it, however, for several years to fortune-500 companies. When they needed technical help, they brought me in, and I did what I could. The fact was that they had developed and sold a prototype, based on a new hardware and software platform, but couldn't deliver the final working system. The reasons are complex and they went all the way back to the failures of some of the biggest name companies in hardware and software history. In any case, I couldn't help them much, but I kept trying. The most heartfelt moments were when I had to meet with customers.

One man in particular I recall who was from a pilot plant that made dog food in Iowa. He called me every day, hoping for a miracle. His company had put $800,000 into the system, and he had been hired to make it work. His employers didn't know a disk from a cable modem, and weren't qualified to make the purchase in the first place (the deal had reportedly been sealed on a private golf course). Unfortunately, there was no way he was ever going to get it to work, because even the guys who designed couldn't do it. I later met with him personally and unofficially, and told him to find another job. He did, and I hope he's happier now than he was then.

All too often, the real culprit is the ignorance of the decision-makers. What they need to do is educate themselves, but sometimes they prefer to sit around and grill their employees, hoping to somehow instill magic in them.

What you are looking for, at least in your immediate supervisor, is someone that understands and sympathizes with your job. If you are an electronics technician, you want someone over you who understands electronics, not an accountant. If you are a computer programmer, you don't want to work for an insurance salesman. It's a simple principle, but an extremely important one for technical people to take to heart.

3. The Product Is Good.

Sadly, the value of the product or service that the company generates rarely can overcome flaws in management or the lack of money. The value of the product is critical to the long-term success of a company, however. Netscape is an obvious example here. The product now contends with the best that Microsoft, the behemoth of the software industry, can muster. But, even Netscape had a pot of money to get them rolling and masterful management by someone who really understood his employees and the industry.

The Rest of Us

Of course, some of us aren't looking for the fast track. We don't want to burn the midnight oil in hopes of having more wealth. What we want is a job we enjoy, day to day, with a regular, steady pace. If this is what you want, you should probably look at larger organizations. The government, of course, is the largest and slowest organization of all.

Correspondingly, it offers the greatest stability and the least opportunity for advancement.

These days, it is almost as hard to find a niche that is comfortable and stable as it is to find a fast track to the big bucks. Large companies frequently undergo take-overs and lay-offs.

In the end, whatever niche you are looking for, your security rests in your own skills and your ability to sell them. You should always be aware of your skills. You should know which ones are going to help land your next job. If you have been working on your marketable skills, things will go much better for you when the music stops and everybody has to find a new chair.

At least you won't be the guy on the pogo-stick.

Chapter Nine

How Close Are You to the Money?

"The more original a discovery, the more obvious it seems afterwards."

--- Arthur Koestler

We have discussed several ways to spot a good job. You are looking for a position that will enhance your marketable skills. You also want a position that fits your capabilities. For example, if you are very persuasive you might want to work in sales.

This chapter examines another angle on how to analyze the value of a given position in an organization. The logic of it goes like this:

> ***Any organization will compensate you more if you are directly involved in making money for the company.***

For example, if you work for a winery and you control the fermenting tanks, you are relatively important, as you are making wine. If you work in sales and you sell wine, you are bringing in money for the company product, so again you are important.

If, however, you are involved in technical support for personal computers, you aren't important. You will never make it rich with this company. You probably will never make it into management, either. Why not?

> ***Because you are too far from the money.***

Most of America's top executives come either from accounting or sales. Why? Because these are the people who either control or gather the money. If you want to maximize your income, you must place yourself as close to the money stream as possible. Preferably, you want to be standing in the middle of it.

For example, if you are a computer programmer, you want to work for a company that sells computer programs. The ones that *you* write, not someone else's. That way, you are like the factory, rather than the factory worker. You don't just keep the production going, *you are the producer*. That makes you important. That makes your salary higher. If you are very good, it matters, as it directly affects the income of the whole company. If, on the other hand, you work as a computer programmer for a winery, you aren't important. Why not?

> ***Because you can't affect the company's income stream.***

Even if you were the best programmer in the world, it wouldn't make much difference. This is why sales people are so important and so well paid in most companies. Sales people generate cash in every organization. Their contribution is clear, measurable and always important.

There is, of course, a backlash effect of being close to the money. The more important your job is to the money stream the more people will pay attention to what you are doing. This means that both your successes and your failures will be magnified. You should only take on the responsibility if you feel that your skills are up to the task.

There can be other negative effects. I have worked under a royalty system for software I've developed. For some years I was getting quarterly checks for a percentage of the gross sales value of my software products. It soon became a major portion of my income. This made me very aware of what was selling and what wasn't. It also made the other programmers take notice of who got which project. Rivalry soon abounded.

The system served as a motivator, but it had the bad effect of putting us into competition. As soon as a new product idea was approved, people would vie for the project if it was something that should easily sell. They would also try to avoid difficult projects with little income potential.

Worse, we soon began to point out the failures of others while crowing about our own successes.

Everything we did became magnified. This is the risk of getting close too the money. Your income will be higher, but life is bound to become more stressful.

The happiest arrangements I've seen concerning large monetary rewards have come in the area of stock options. If you can get close enough to the money and you work for a fast-track company, this is the best way to make it rich in technical work.

The plan usually is based upon the annual salary of the individual. The more you make the more stock you will later have the right to buy. Each year that you work with the company, you will gain the right to purchase stock later at a fixed, low price. Then, if the company does well and goes public, you can buy the stock and resell it at a great profit. The better the company does, the better you will do.

This works well as it gives everyone the incentive to work together for the greater good of the team. Rather than the competition generated by sales commissions and royalties, it tends to increase teamwork. If the company goes down, everyone goes down with it. If the company wins, everyone wins.

That is, everyone who was close enough to the money wins. In most cases, clerical people and others won't be allowed to participate. They aren't important enough to the success of the company.

Early on in your career, the main thing to think about is how to judge a new job. If you want to maximize your income, you must be in a key position at the company. You must be as close to the money stream as possible.

For example, if you are a technical trainer, you will probably do best working for a company that specializes in technical trainings. If you are a networking specialist, you will tend to make more at a network installation company than at a bank. If you are a biochemist, work for a biochemical company, rather than a food-processing company.

Always remember, however, to balance the stresses and risks of any job against the potential rewards. Many start-up companies make vague promises about everyone getting rich later. Make sure that the path to this goal is clear and believable. Also:

Make sure these promises are in writing.

Chapter Ten
Management Cultures

"If you truly want to understand something, try to change it."

--- Kurt Lewin

The background of the people largely drives the culture of management at a given organization involved. Many companies have unwritten and often unspoken traditions that dictate who they recruit as new executives. Primarily, they tend to hire from among their own kind.

What kind? If they are accountants, they hire more accountants. If they are sales people, they hire more sales people. If they are engineers or entrepreneurs, they find others like themselves.

In the United States, accountants run most organizations. For technical people, this may be alarming, but it is true. Any government agency is a clear example of this type of organization. Second in line are the sales-driven types such as IBM. Third and last are the engineering types. In any field other than the technical areas, engineers don't run anything, but they do have a stake in technical work. Apple Computers is an example of a company that was run by technical people for many years.

If you are serious about a company and a position, it is a good idea to learn who is at the top and how they think. Each of these three management cultures has its pros and cons.

It's useful to study how and why these cultures evolved. First come the accountants. Clearly, they are close to the money. Who could be closer than the person who prints out the balance sheet?

Accountants have come into power by holding the purse strings tightly. One would think that executives could and would simply disregard the opinion of the accountants in some cases. If, for example, your plant manager is telling you that they need new workstations to raise production, you should believe it, right? After all, who is in the best position to know?

It is reasonable to ask your accountant: "Can we afford that this month?" That is the job of the accountant, to know how much money you have and where you are spending it. Unfortunately, the accountants tend to take their jobs too seriously and begin to color their responses with their own ideas.

The way they look at it, the old workstations are still running. That is good enough.

Request denied.

That very act of denying requests has, contrary to all good sense, brought accountants to unrivaled power in many corporations.

Another factor contributing to their power is the "king and counselor" relationship that tends to develop between the executive and the accountant. Often, only the accountants are trusted with the company's balance sheets. Only the accountants know where the money is truly being spent. This closeness and familiarity tends to get them into management.

The size of organizations is also a factor. As organizations get larger and more complex, the easiest way to manage them is from the balance sheet. Decisions can be made more easily if you reduce all choices to numbers, percentages and monthly flows. There is little risk involved that way, but also little flexibility.

One hot July I was working with a team of ten engineers in a large open lab. On the first of the month, we noticed that a locked plastic box had appeared over the thermostat that controlled the air conditioner. The thermostat was set for eighty degrees and we couldn't change it.

Now, eighty degrees isn't unbearable, but it is enough to annoy most people. Computers and people generate heat of their own, which added to the situation. Some of our larger people were sweating profusely.

After a couple of days like this, I decided to act. As I was the engineering manager, I made a few phone calls but only got voicemail. Using an old college trick, I attacked the shielded thermostat with keys and a pen. In time, I managed to set the temperature to seventy-two. Everyone sighed in relief.

But the next day, it was back up to eighty. As the day warmed up, the president of the company came by to check on us. Immediately, he complained about the heat. I explained the situation.

He became unglued. He picked up the phone and demanded the presence of the company controller. The man made his appearance. The president asked for an explanation. We all stood there, watching. Some of us grinned. We knew our president and his intolerance of misguided accountants.

The man completely missed the mood of the crowd. He explained proudly and animatedly that he had discovered a way to save the company better than $300 a month. All he had to do was raise the thermostat setting. He proclaimed this to be his cost-cutting brainchild of the year.

Our president was dumbfounded. "Don't you realize that each of these employees cost us four to five thousand a month?" he demanded. "If you have reduced their effectiveness even slightly, this is a huge waste of money."

Actually, he said things that were a lot worse, but I won't repeat them here. The technical people won that day because our executive was an entrepreneur, not an accountant.

Not all controllers are that bad, but as a rule:

They tend to see only expenses, not the value of what those expenses are buying.

I've been flown around the country as much as seven extra hours to save a hundred bucks on airfare. Very recently, I was turned down for a project because I didn't have the low bid, even though I could reduce a company's operating costs by enough to finance the whole project in the first month of operation.

Companies run by accountants aren't always bad, but in the technical field they are generally the worst. This is because they aren't flexible, and can't adapt easily to the never-ending storm that is technology. They tend to be more interested in corporate mergers and cost cutting than researching a new product. This can spell doom in the age of technology.

Second on the list are the sales-driven companies. These are better for our purposes. They tend to follow money like bloodhounds. Sales is what matters to them, the movement of products out the door. Costs are secondary to income. Their approach is to make more money rather than to spend less.

Unfortunately, sales-driven companies can make more spectacular errors than other types of companies. They are more prone to waste money and make mistakes that result in lay-offs. They understand risks and are willing to take them, but don't have the technical know-how to judge which risks to take. Another unfortunate tendency is for them to become arrogant in this culture. They often seem to believe that since they are the ones bringing home the bacon, everyone else is more or less a drone.

I recall one conversation vividly. After working at an IBM installation in Florida for a month or so, I was approached by a senior manager. I had been doing sales support and technical presentations. He liked my work and wanted me to do sales work for IBM directly. He said that I was clearly too much of a people-person to stick with technical work.

I politely declined, saying that while I could sell, it wasn't really my career goal. He pushed, of course, as salespeople will. I remained polite, but firm.

Finally, in exasperation, he demanded, "I don't understand this! Do you want to be a *techie* for the rest of your life?"

His arrogance angered me, but I did my best to hide it, as he was actually my customer at the time. I told him that I had spent a long time in college getting a bachelor and a master's degree in computer science. I explained that I liked being a software engineer and that I saw myself as a craftsman.

I'm not sure if he ever understood. His company culture put sales at the top. He had great difficulty with the idea of any thinking person who didn't want to join him at the top.

The third major type of management culture is probably the wildest. True entrepreneurs who have a technical background can sometimes make it big. Apple Computers and companies like it are obvious examples.

These companies definitely have their own cultures. Often, they tend to be "personality" companies. That is, they reflect the attitudes and beliefs of the person at the top. This is usually a mixed bag for the employee. If the company president is a bit of a nut, the company will do slightly nutty things.

Although I've never worked for Apple, I've heard plenty of stories about their operations. For example, when they were coming out with the Macintosh, Steve Jobs decided that the footprint of the computer couldn't be any larger than a phonebook. By "footprint" he meant how large the box was, how much space it took up on the surface of the desk. He just decided this arbitrarily, based on the idea that people would like a computer of that size.

Personal computers of the day were much larger than this. Reducing the size meant many technical problems. For one thing, the circuit boards would have to be compressed. For another, there would be problems with heat build-up. Steve didn't care. His order was a mandate that couldn't be argued with.

History is ambivalent as to whether or not he was right, but that isn't the point. The point is that technical leadership is a double-edged sword for the technical employee. On the good side, you've got someone in management who understands and respects you. On the bad side, you've got someone who has their own ideas about how your job should be done. This means they may well try to micro-manage you. You might end up with less freedom rather than more.

There are other pros and cons as well. Technical people who manage companies tend not to be as good at business. They are split between two fields, and their business decisions tend to be less sound. On the up side, however, they are able to recognize the future trends of technology more quickly and take advantage of them.

There is another, new cultural element to management that is being talked about everywhere I go. This is a beast called: TQM. TQM stands for Total Quality Management. Currently, it is a favorite buzzword nation-wide.

TQM originates from the business management theories of W. Edwards Demming. Japanese manufacturing companies were the first to subscribe to these theories. They owe a significant part their success to TQM.

There are many books based on TQM, so I won't give you the whole story here. In a nutshell, TQM suggests that the old management structures are outdated. It says that management should involve the whole company in its decisions, rather than just a few members at the top who talk behind closed doors. The idea is that if everyone in the company is involved in as many decisions as possible, all the employees will feel more committed to the company. Since companies are really dependent upon the individual performance of their employees, if they feel satisfied with the way things are going, everyone will be happier. Everyone will do a better job and the company will prosper.

In a manufacturing environment, quality is assured from the top to the bottom of the operation. Much of this is done by statistical analysis, comparing the quality of raw materials against the finished product, for instance.

For purposes of manufacturing, it is unquestionable that many companies have employed TQM principles with great results. More recently, however, corporations have tried to apply these same principles to other types of industry. At first glance, this sounds good. And I'm sure there are some model companies out there that have taken this to heart and are making it work.

Unfortunately, the attempts at implementation outside of manufacturing that I've witnessed firsthand have been miserable failures. This is primarily because productivity and quality are difficult to measure without a real product. If an automobile manufacturing company employs TQM, they can easily measure the quality of their automobiles vs. the steel it took to make them, for example. An insurance company, however, has no real basis for these measurements. If two $100,000 life insurance policies are sold, each for the same premium, which is better in quality? The question is nonsensical, there is no tangible reality to either policy, and therefore no way to measure or compare quality.

Because of this fundamental flaw, the application of TQM outside of manufacturing is rarely successful. Without quality measurement, TQM becomes only a change in the way that a company is managed. This means that the biggest changes must occur in management itself. The problems begin when the TQM concept runs up against the three much older and more ingrained cultures I've laid out above. If you are working for a place run by purse-clutching accountants, arrogant salespeople or wild-eyed entrepreneurs, there is a problem:

None of them are about to give up any real power.

Oh sure, there will be lip-service given to the TQM concept. Seminars will be held. Everyone will have more meetings. The exact layout of the breakroom might even be discussed and decided upon by everyone.

With meetings and dispersed power everywhere, the job of middle managers becomes a nightmare. They find that what little power they had to make decisions has been eroded further by the natural squabbling of everyone around them with an opinion.

Outside of manufacturing, technical people are usually in trouble with TQM. This is especially true if they work in an environment where they are not well understood. Since they aren't understood, they are often disliked and feared. They represent change.

Using TQM, everyone is supposed to have meetings and talk out everything. Management might believe that this is everyone's chance to learn why the changes are needed. Instead, all too often, what happens is that the less technical types think of it as a chance to explain why the changes shouldn't occur. They believe that here is their chance to stop the changes. This is their opportunity to make the others see reason.

Of course, they really have no choice. Management is just trying to be gentle about it. In doing so, they give everyone false hope. When their objections are ignored, management is perceived as having misled everyone. They appear to be playing games. When you get to this point you have more contention, rather than less.

I have lived with TQM in several non-manufacturing organizations. I've never seen it solve anything. Instead, it has caused problems.

In the end, the problem with TQM is that it requires the people in power to relinquish some of their power voluntarily. Unfortunately, this is contrary to human nature. People like power. That is why they work so hard to get it.

If you are dealing with TQM in a non-manufacturing workplace, you may or may not suffer the same results that I have. I caution you, however, about speaking out against TQM even if you do find it counterproductive. In the nineties business climate, it is not a good idea. TQM has become a religion among many of its followers. I recommend that you don't reject their false idol, as you may well be labeled a heretic.

Simply smile, nod and wait it out. Eventually, it will fade, or it may begin to really work. As a rule, management fads that are designed to generate seminars tend to burn out after a few years.

Chapter Eleven
Family Kingdoms

"A little nepotism can go a long way."

--- Dan Larson

There is one more common type of management culture worth discussing. I've set it apart from those laid out in the previous chapter, as it is really a layer that can be added to any of the other management cultures. I'm referring, of course, to the family-owned business.

Family businesses are privately owned. The company stock in most cases is not open for public trading. All the stock, or at least the majority of it, is privately held, usually by the members of a single family. This means that as long as the company doesn't go public and doesn't sell too much stock to investors, it can't be taken over by anyone outside of the owning family.

Besides the special cultural tendencies of family-owned businesses, which I will discuss here, the company can have a management culture of accountancy, sales or entrepreneurship. Entrepreneurs are commonly found in charge of this type of company.

Families run many businesses, large and small. It a more common phenomenon for smaller companies but exists for any size of company. Families can run anything from mom and pop grocery stores to giant billion-dollar corporations.

I've actually spent many years working for family-owned and operated companies. I've also had the opportunity to deal with and talk to people who have had similar experiences working for other family-owned businesses. This has given me a special insight into the idiosyncrasies of the family-owned business.

The Strengths of Family Businesses

1. The People Running The Place Really Care.

Whether they are right or wrong about any decision, if the people in upper management own the company they will care what happens to it. Every decision they make will directly affect their own personal fortunes. Their job isn't just five days a week, it is often the major focus of their lives.

2. As Long As The Family Owns The Company, Management Will Rarely Change.

How many of us have taken a job only to learn soon after that the manager we liked so much is gone? If you like your job and your management, you will find things more stable at a family-owned company. Managers will be less likely to leave if they are part of a ruling family. Management structures in family businesses are often very rigid.

3. You Can Do Very Well If You Are In Favor With The Family.

If you are a member of the family, even a distant relation, or if you are simply liked by some powerful member, you can do very well. One of the quickest ways to rise in a company is association with a ruling family. It's not fair, but it works.

4. Often, There Is A More Personable Atmosphere.

Many family-run businesses can be fun, caring places to work. Some owners treat their employees as members of their extended family. This is more common with smaller companies.

5. A Family-Run Company That Makes It Big Can Often Be Generous.

If you grow with the company over the years, the rewards may be greater than if you did so with more business-like management. Professional managers will often see an employee's salary as reward enough, no matter what contribution they have made. This all depends on the family involved, of course.

6. In Some Cases, The Family May Prefer To Stay Out Of Management.

In what is usually the best scenario, family members might be willing to sit back like modern English royalty and let the professionals do their jobs. If they choose their top executives well, this is an excellent arrangement for everyone. In my experience, however, this sort of arrangement is the exception rather than the rule.

The Downside

1. Many Families Run Their Companies Like Personal Kingdoms.

The structure of any family-run business concentrates all the power in one small group of people. These people are then akin to royalty in their own company. There is often no oversight from a board of directors. There are no public shareholders with the right to complain. This means that if a manager is bad, there is may be no getting rid of him or her.

Mary, a friend of mine, worked as a personnel manager in one such company/kingdom. The company provided cable TV service over a large area. Due to a very lucrative near-monopoly, what had started as a mom and pop place decades ago had grown into a major corporation.

One day Mary received an emergency call from the owner and was ordered to drop everything and drive out to their estate. She canceled two appointments and walked out on a third with apologies. When she finally got to the house, an hour's drive away, she learned the nature of the emergency: the owner's wife had lost her earrings.

2. The Leadership Is Often Less Well-Educated, Less Experienced And Less Professional.

The criteria for running an office might be that you are Bill's niece. No other applicants need apply. This works well if Bill's niece is competent. All too frequently, she will not be.

3. At Some Point, The Head Of The Family Will Die.

In every kingdom, there is a point of crisis built into the system. That crisis comes when the king or queen dies. What do you do then? If there is no clear ascension to the throne, then war might be the result. Businesses war with weapons called: lawyers.

4. The New Head Of The Company Will Rarely Be As Good As The First.

Unfortunately, virtue isn't hereditary. Often, the rich kid or the befuddled spouse of the dead monarch isn't up to the job. They didn't build the company up from the ground. They didn't follow their dreams, work hard and achieve success. They were born into, or they married into, wealth. In most cases, this means they will either sell out for what they can get, or they run the place into the ground with bad management.

5. If You Aren't "In" With The Family, You Will Never Rise To The Top.

Family members are royalty, and they bestow nobility upon their friends. Anyone else is a commoner.

6. Sometimes The Monarch's Butler Has More Power Than Any Vice President.

As in any kingdom, proximity to the royalty is more important than any title. This can be quite frustrating for professionals who aren't interested in, or aren't allowed to, hob-nob with the royalty.

7. Hatchet-Men And Hatchet-Women Tend To Arise.

All too often one individual will gain proximity to, and thus the ear of, the monarch. This person may well not even be part of management. When this happens, personal vendettas can mean the jobs of many people. More than once I've witnessed this phenomenon occur with the monarch and the monarch's secretary or spouse.

I've seen companies where the owner's butler, secretary or spouse elicited great fear from employees. Just the mention of the person's name brought everyone, even executives, to full alert.

8. Swearing Loyalty to the Crown

As you can see, there is quite a list of positives and negatives. Each company is different, as each family is different. In most cases, there is a mixed bag of pros and cons. You must judge the company as best you can and see if it is the place you want to work.

As a final note, you should remember that smaller companies are more affected by family management than larger companies. This is because one family can only be stretched so far. Larger corporations can't be completely managed by just one small group of people. Consequently, they have a powerful majority of professional managers. Most employees will never deal with the ruling elite directly.

Smaller companies, however, suffer from the reverse situation. Often there are more family members around than there are top management positions. The ruling family will be present at every meeting and dealing with them will be inescapable.

Chapter Twelve
Self-Employment

"I am a great believer in luck and I find the harder I work the more I have of it."

--- Stephen Leacock

Many people dream of self-employment. On the surface, it looks pretty good. Depending on the demand that exists for whatever service or product you are providing to the public, the sky is the limit on earnings. You make your own hours and set your own goals.

Self-employment is the very essence of capitalism. You work for yourself and technically no one is your boss. You may even have employees and be the boss yourself.

There are many things to be considered before going into business for yourself, however:

1. The Customer Is Always Right.

If you have any difficulty getting along with your current employers, self-employment isn't the answer.

If you start your own business, you will that you find you have not one, but many bosses. They are called customers.

In reality, as a self-employed person almost everyone is your boss. You want to trade them goods and services for their money. This means you must be nice to them. This means you must do what they say.

I've known a few people who had the technical skills, but not the people skills, to make it on their own. This can be disheartening, but illuminating. One thing is for sure, if you try self-employment for a year or two, you won't view a boss in quite the same way ever again.

2. Without Sales, You Will Quickly Go Broke.

Perhaps the most critical skill that technical people fail to take into consideration when they step out on their own is their sales ability. Often, they get started with a single contract that all but falls into their laps. Or, they might have come into a pot of money and be anxious to try their hand at building a business with it. Working alone, you are the only salesperson. You must have more sales to survive.

If you are working hourly contracts, for example, this means that you must constantly get new contracts. This is rather like going through the job-hunting and hiring process we've discussed on a continuous basis.

3. Self-Employment Is Rarely Less Work.

Some people become infatuated with the idea of collecting all the money from their labors. What they forget is that the salespeople, accountants, receptionists, etc. are all working. With all of them gone, you, the only person in your organization, has to fill all these roles. Most self-employed people work long hard hours with few breaks.

4. Taxes Are Higher.

Self-employed people must pay double what most of us do to social security. This comes to a hefty sum. There are no deductions, it is a flat rate. Always calculate that extra 7.5% into your hourly rate when considering a contract. Additionally, there will be various licenses and fees for operating a business. Most of the income tax reductions that businesses used to enjoy for expenses are now gone.

5. Sometimes, People Forget To Pay You.

One of the worst things that can happen to any small business occurs when their clients don't pay. This can come from any of a variety of reasons, but tends to happen more when you really need the money. Some companies make a regular habit of squeezing their small suppliers and contractors when they get a chance to.

The smaller you are, the more likely you are to get squeezed as you are less important to them, and less able to defend yourself in court. I've seen every kind of nightmare. Checks coming in 30, 60 or 90 days late. After 120 days, maybe they pay 30% of the balance. Most companies pay their bills, but not always on time.

Getting Started

A friend of mine named Mike got out of the military and landed a job working for a computer networking company. He soon found that he wasn't happy with his job. After some months he was handed a self-employed contract out of the blue. The contract offered six months of work for a food-processing company installing a computer network. Making $50 an hour sounded pretty good, so he quit his regular job and worked the contract. He told me he planned to take a few months off afterwards to nail down the next contract, and so on. He figured he could work only half the year and still make a good living.

It didn't work out that way. The first contract ended early after only four months. Jobless and without any leads for the next job, he beat on doors without success for several more months. He learned one of the hard lessons of job-hunting:

> **It's much easier to get a new job when you already have one.**

Determined to succeed, he stuck it out and finally got another contract. By that time people were on the phone threatening to repo his car, his house, everything. He worked the second contract and before that one was done, got another.

In fact, he never stopped looking for the next contract. Starvation had taught him what every stray dog knows: always look for food, and if you see some, eat it immediately. In his case of course, it was work he was looking for, not food.

His improved sales efforts finally reaped great rewards and soon he was working night and day, seven days a week. He began to hire people and a new company was born.

Mike's story is very typical. In many forms of technical work, it can be difficult to work at a steady pace. Sometimes work will flood in, at other times no one will buy anything. Most of the successful self-employed people that I know work incredible hours and rarely take vacations.

The keys to success are those I've already laid out in previous chapters. You need three elements: a reserve money supply, smart management and a quality service or product that is in demand. If there is a fourth element, it is the ability to sell.

There are three major types of products and services a small business can offer:

1. Most People Start With Service.

The most common beginning business for technical work is contracting. By the way, you should always call contracting "consulting". It sounds better and will usually allow you to charge more. Consulting consists of selling your skills and services to a company or individual who wants them. It is often done on a per-hour or per-day basis. It is similar to having a short-term job.

Consulting has advantages. First, you can usually do it by yourself and collect all the money. Second, it takes almost no materials or capital to get started, just a contract. This means you can start immediately.

2. New Businesses Often Move Next Into Reselling.

Reselling is the classic business of buying low and selling high. Many new businesses find that their customers would like to purchase not just service but also products from them. This can be quite lucrative, as it allows the reseller to purchase at wholesale prices and resell at retail prices.

One of my relatives runs his own pool service. He found soon after starting that people wanted him to supply all their pool needs, including new pumps, filters, etc. Buying these at a big discount allows him to make money on every sale.

There are a few negative points to being a reseller. One is the paperwork. Another is the need to maintain some form of inventory and the urge to buy in bulk to save money. Buying in bulk only saves money when you can sell what you buy.

3. A Company Can Produce and Sell Its Own Products.

This, of course, is the top of the hill. It is quite difficult to do, however. It usually takes a company of significant size to produce and sell its own products. Consultants and resellers are common beginnings, but inventing your own product usually takes a much larger investment of time and money. Often, it is impossible without employees.

Growth

You may have heard that to survive, a company must grow and adapt. There is much truth to this. We have already examined in depth why any technical firm must adapt constantly to keep up with technology. But often, a company must grow, too. Without growth, it can be difficult to get work. Any new area of work that you might discover a niche in will usually be discovered by others, too. They will compete with you, and eventually the one that grows into the most successful corporation wins. As a one-man-show, it can be difficult to compete.

It is almost impossible to compete if you stay small with a product-based company. As a reseller, it is easier, but eventually some chain will come along and wipe out all the little mom and pop places. As a lone contractor, it is possible to stay in for a very long time. But even doctors these days can't go it alone any more. They've turned into something called: HMOs.

Eventually, you will be faced with the choice of growing or dying. Growth means employees, and a whole new set of opportunities and headaches. At that point many people find they've become business people and are no longer practicing their technical skills. Someday you may find yourself at the head of an entrepreneur-run company or a family kingdom of your own.

Contract Negotiations

Depending on the nature of the work, contract negotiations can be critical. If a company is just offering to hire you for a prescribed length of time to work for them, there is little to worry about. It is when you are asked for a bid, an estimate of how long and for how much you can complete a project that things can go badly. When negotiating a contract for the first time, here are some things to be consider:

1. Don't Under-Bid.

If you are asked to bid on a large project that is at all unclear, be cautious. Companies will often push for a fixed price contract that says you will do X for Y. This means that you could end up working for a year on a project you thought would take six months. In this situation, for the last six months you will effectively be working for free.

2. Don't Over-Bid.

There will almost always be a competitor, even if they don't tell you about it. This competitor will know about you and do what they can to stop you from getting the contract. Since this is true, don't overprice yourself.

3. Turn A Large Project Into Several Small Stages.

One of the keys to large unclear projects is staged development. This is a series of steps—*paid* steps—each with its own price tag and its own clear end-point.

Most of the contracts I've written involved software development for factory automation. Like most technical work, this is a tricky area with many opportunities for something to go wrong. My standard first stage in large projects consists of a week's consulting time to investigate the project and write a detailed proposal for a new system. This usually is a good deal for the customer, as it clarifies what they wanted to do without much commitment. At the same time, it allows me to figure out just how much work is involved, what they really want, etc.

After the investigation phase, I continue to break off chunks and attach price tags to them. At each step, it is critical that they get something useful. With this deliverable, of course, they get your proposed bid for completion of the next stage. This system reduces the risk of financial loss on both sides.

4. Be Careful About Liability.

You should maintain liability insurance on your own. This is by far the safest course, but you can also try to get a liability clause in your contract, basically making the company liable for whatever you do.

Always remember that we in the U.S. have ten times the number of lawyers that Japan has per capita and one-fourth the number of engineers. By my calculations, this makes it about forty times more likely for you or me to get sued in this country.

5. Look Out For Big Companies With Big Promises.

Many larger companies crush, staple and mutilate smaller companies with idle promises. I could name several specific examples, but I won't due to the forty-odd lawyers that are waiting out there for me. Let's give you a little story instead:

Let's say you've developed a new product that sells well as an add-on to an existing product from a big company. In time, your product proves itself. You build up your company and after a year or two you've got fifty employees.

Now Big Red Inc. comes along and casually mentions a multi-million dollar buyout. They say they want to see just how good your stuff is. They talk about "due-diligence" and "quality-audits". They buy a few units of your product and mention millions more orders in an off-handed way.

This is your dream scenario. You are going to be rich. Everyone in the company is going to make out like bandits. Your spouse is very excited and has brochures of Tahiti laid out all over the coffee table. All of your hard work and sacrifice is going to finally pay off in a big way.

You invite them in. Teams of people in expensive suits thoroughly investigate your company from the inside. They go over your books, your accounts, and your technology.

Then, a month later, the deal sours. Someone calls you on the phone to apologize and tell you something just came up and they have no more millions. The people in the suits vanish into the twilight.

Six months later Big Red Inc. announces a new breakthrough product. They claim no one has seen the like of it. You take one look at it and recognize it immediately. It is your product, repackaged and renamed.

So you decide to sue. They counter-sue. They have ten times the number of lawyers you do, and theirs are smarter. The courts grind on for years, but by that time you have gone broke, your spouse left for Tahiti without you and you ran out of money to pay your own lawyers. Six years later, you get them to settle out of court for enough to buy yourself a fast-food fish sandwich.

No fries.

This horror story, or a variation of it, has occurred many times. I've witnessed these things firsthand. The key is not to let larger companies lead you on with promises of wealth untold. You might get it, but you will be more likely to if you play it smart and make them pay as they go along.

Remember, they didn't get big by playing Santa Claus.

In the end, what you really want to do in a new business is get a list of steady customers you can work with. Chasing big deals all the time can look inviting, but often it is the smaller, steady money that keeps you going. If you can build a working rapport with a set of customers by doing good work for them at a competitive price, you will succeed. Watch out for companies that want to squeeze you with your own greed. Some of them make a regular habit of this behavior.

Then again, you might decide to forget self-employment altogether. That leads into the next chapter, where we'll study approaches for making the most out of your job choices.

Chapter Thirteen
Job-Hopping

"The hardest thing in life to learn is which bridge to cross and which to burn."

--- David Russell

Job-hopping is the *excessive* switching of jobs. Everyone switches jobs now and then, it is expected. In fact, staying in one place for too long is a disadvantage in the job market rather than an advantage.

How long is *too* long? More than ten years is too long. At that point, you aren't an engineer—you become an IBM engineer, for example.

Everyone switches jobs, but it can be overdone. As an employer, I considered anyone a job-hopper who regularly switched jobs once a year or more. Most employers don't like job-hoppers because they are more likely to leave when you need them. There is a lot of work and expense involved in hiring someone. Even after finding the right person, there is a training period before a new hire is able to do useful work. In technical fields this training period is longer, and subsequently more expensive, than in other areas.

However, there are times that you should leave a job even when you haven't been there very long. Don't fear being labeled a job-hopper so much that you stick with something you truly dislike. Often, people get forced into job-hopping because they take jobs they shouldn't have. Perhaps their working conditions are intolerable on their new job. Maybe they learn that they just aren't qualified for the position. Or perhaps they are getting paid less than they had understood.

When to Consider a Job-Hop

The hardest part about job-hopping is deciding when to do it.

1. If Things Are Awful on a New Job, Quit Early.

Don't hang around for six months or a year to make it look good. If the situation is really bad, and you are confident you can get something else, then quit. You aren't doing anyone any good by hanging around before you quit. That only means that the company wasted more money on your training before you left them.

If you worked for just a few months, consider dropping the item entirely from your resume. That way, you appear just to be searching carefully, not job-hopping. Don't leave too long of a gap between employment, however. Six months or so will look like you are too fussy or that you aren't getting any offers.

Possibly, you may want to search for a new job before you leave your present one. This is tricky, but often it is much easier to get a new job while you are working. People like the idea of taking you away from someone else. If you are jobless, it appears that you aren't as hot of an item. (This isn't true, of course, but people tend to think this way.)

2. Jumping When You Get a Better Offer.

This is somewhat more risky. You must be very certain of the offer. Get it in writing, and then quit. Remember, though, that the grass isn't always greener on the other side. It is not always possible to go back to your old company and beg forgiveness. Even if you do get back in, you will have lost points with management.

Jim, an excellent engineer fresh out of college, worked with me at a job for about a year. While at a customer site, he was informally offered more money to come work for them. This was seen as a betrayal by our management, as he had made the deal while on the job. He took it, without really knowing much about the position. He soon found he didn't like it, and hopped again. Two years and four hops later, he ended up coming back to the first company. His salary and position were somewhat higher, but he was never trusted or looked upon in the same way by management again.

3. When You Can See Your Present Company Sliding Down Into The Abyss.

Often in the modern age technology companies boom and bust. When they start to bust, usually the first people to know it are the employees. Your value is directly connected to the value of the company you work for. If it becomes rich and powerful, your status is elevated. If it goes broke, people will think less of you.

Since we can only rarely make or break a company by ourselves, we are all basically helpless in the face of such booms and busts. All we can do is time things correctly.

Your stock as an employee is tied to the stock of the company you work for: *so you should sell when it's high.* When you see it begin to go down, this is a good time to jump ship. If you do it early enough, people in other companies won't know yet that there is a problem and will be more likely to hire you.

The Up-Side of Job-Hopping

It's easy to see the negative side of job-hopping, so let's examine the positive. The odd truth is that to maximize your career-climb, you will probably need to switch jobs. This is especially true in the technical fields. On average, I've seen people do the best by staying with each job for at least a year, but not more than five. In fact, most of the rapid rises in salary and position I've seen have come to people that switched about every two years.

How can this be? Whatever happened to working your way up a corporate ladder?

It still happens. Corporate ladders exist and to reach the very top of some companies, you must climb one. But, there is very often an undisclosed shortcut to the top. This is made by coming in from the outside.

When you are hired into a company from the outside, people judge you in those first few weeks or months. People like to put everything in a category, so you will be put into one. If you do great things your first week, then you become a "doer". People might call you "proactive". If you are hired in as a service technician and you do a fair job of it that is what you become in the minds of everyone in that company. It soon becomes unthinkable that you would do anything else. There are only a few points at which you might break out of that description.

One we have already discussed, the excuse of higher education is one of these points. If you get a new degree, the odds are better that you can climb the ladder another notch or move to a new ladder—going from equipment operation to technical training, for example. Or you may move from technical service to sales.

But in most cases, companies like to hire a manager from somewhere else rather than to promote from within. New hires are different, somehow. No one knows who or what he or she is, so they seem intriguing, new and special. Have you ever noticed how video rental places charge twice as much for "new arrivals"? Next year, they'll just be old has-beens. Junk that everybody has seen. Freshness has power in the job market, too.

Oddly enough, people are as impressed with those that get away and join another company as those that come in from the outside. When you leave, they look up at you in surprise and say,

"My, she just got a better job. She must be someone special."

Sometimes the only way to keep expanding your skills and moving towards your career goals is to switch jobs. If they won't promote you, you can promote yourself by finding an employer who will give you the chance.

My own wife, now an information systems specialist, has made a thoughtful series of job-switches. Before she finished her degree, Alma first worked for a very large company as a receptionist. She did well and was well liked, but was never considered for advancement. She moved on to work as a computer operator for a second, smaller company. Again she did well, but was stuck in that position. She left that job after a time and went back to the first company, now working in technical maintenance, assembling and trouble-shooting computer hardware. She tried to advance into technical training, but was overlooked. Finishing her degree in information systems, she switched back to the second company, becoming their network administrator.

This process has been going on for years, and as of this date, the odyssey continues. Along the way, Alma finished her degree and made friends with everyone she could in both companies. Somehow, she has managed to seem new, unknown and interesting several times over to the same companies.

One premise that has helped her is that it is easier to rise in a smaller company than a larger one. Unfortunately, smaller ones don't pay as much. Therefore, the role of the smaller ones is to help you get the type of job you want, thus providing you the experience and skills you need. Once you have that, getting into the larger company with these new skills is far easier. There, you will be better compensated for these new skills that the larger company would otherwise never have allowed you to gain.

Applying this approach repeatedly, I've no doubt that Alma will end up running both of these companies someday.

PART III: KEEPING YOUR JOB AND MOVING UP

Chapter Fourteen
Surviving Your New Job

"Business is war."

--- Modern Japanese Proverb

Up until this point, the book has focused upon preparing oneself for a technical career and landing a job in your field. Now I shall assume you have that job. How do you keep it? How do you advance? These are the questions the following chapters will answer.

First of all, let's discuss expectations. If you want a cush and easy job—in case you haven't already figured it out—you shouldn't bother with a technical career. This isn't the fifties. To make it in the modern workplace, it takes more than a degree, more than showing up on time, more than just looking busy. In fact, it is often necessary to skip lunches, eating only a quick bite at your desk. You will have to work after five, and before eight. Weekends, nights and even days off may get intruded upon from time to time.

There is no such thing as a nine-to-five job. I actually expected my first job out of college would be nine-to-five—imagine my surprise! I don't know why people still say nine-to-five these days. Even the bankers are working longer hours now.

People in this country work eight-to-five and then start adding hours from there. This is true for everyone, but is particularly true for people in technical work.

Not only are the hours tough, but also the workplace is definitely a tenser environment than it was just a few decades ago. I wish that things were easier, but they aren't, and the situation isn't going to change for many years. Robert B. Reich, former Secretary of Labor, speaking to Louis Uchitelle of the *New York Times*, said it this way: "Worker-management relations today are very tense, given all the corporate downsizings, the increased litigation in the workplace, the technological changes and the enormous pressures on companies to cut costs."

I recall one of my professors in college telling us that we would probably never have to work as hard at a job as we worked at school. Computer Science is a very difficult major in college and there was some truth to the statement then. It doesn't hold water today, however.

There is less focus upon learning, but there are many new pressures and long hours that make work far more stressful than school. Going to school lets you set your own pace and schedule for the most part. You decide how many classes to take. You decide when and if to study for a test, and for how long. If you get a B instead of an A, no one is going to throw you out of school and cut off your income. On the other hand, when we are working, supervisors decide how much we can and should get done. They also decide when it is overdue. Worse, they have the power to enforce their decisions.

During the early nineties I was working full-time as a technical manager and taking one or two night-classes at a time towards my master's degree. Suddenly, there was a crisis at work. Several important customers were demanding a major overhaul of our software products, and they wanted it yesterday. This was nothing new, but management's approach to solving it was.

We were ordered into a locked pit for six weeks. For six weeks, eight engineering people were placed in a single large room around a single large table. We were to work for six days a week, twelve hours a day, *at least*. All meals would be brought in: breakfast, lunch and dinner. All eating was to be done over a keyboard.

At the end, if everyone's work were done, we'd get a cash bonus of around five thousand dollars each.

As it turned out, we spent more than twelve hours a day trapped in that room. Some of us slept on the floors. At all hours of the night someone was there, clicking at the keyboard and swearing.

There were personality conflicts as fatigue and general cabin fever set in. There were arguments about what kind of music to play, so much so that finally our boss bought everyone their own CD player, with headphones. There were marital problems. My wife, swearing not to leave until I did, spent a night on the floor in protest. One of the programmers fell in love with another, and was spurned. Another took to slashing the tires of management in the parking lot.

In the end, I made it through the experience, retaining my job, education and marriage. All three were threatened, however. I do hope that none of you have to go through similar experiences, but I want you to know they do occur. If you are single, hot on your job, hungry for money and young, this sort of thing can be a fun challenge. Otherwise, it can be a form of hell.

What If Things Go Right?

Let's assume your new job is reasonable to you. It should be if you have chosen carefully, taking into consideration all the factors discussed in the previous chapters. Hopefully, you have measured the quality and culture of the management, the abundance of the money supply and the value of the product or service. If it is a smaller company, you have made sure the risks of working there are balanced by the better potential rewards. If it is a large organization, you can see your career path clearly and know what skills you will be gaining to enhance your career while walking that path.

Even if you have chosen well, there is a list of things you should do immediately to ease your transition into a new environment.

1. Find One Or More Mentors.

Many new companies assign you a mentor upon joining them. Too often, however, this person is your busy supervisor who doesn't have time to show you the ropes. Maybe they are even about to leave for two weeks to Europe on your first day of the job (this happened to me a few years ago.) If you aren't assigned a mentor, or the one you are assigned isn't helpful, you must find another.

Sometimes you need several mentors for different areas. You may need someone to explain the technical details of your work, someone to explain the company politics and perhaps another to help you choose the best financial options on your benefits package. The key to finding mentors is finding people who are willing to talk, and what they want to talk about. If you find their favorite topic, and always bring it up and listen attentively, people are fountains of critical information.

If you find people aren't interested in telling you things, clam up and move on to someone else, unless you are desperate.

2. Find Out Who Your Supervisor Is.

It may seem strange, but many people start work not knowing exactly whom they work for. This is especially true for new positions that haven't been fit into the organizational structure yet. You may be told that you work for several people, in which case you should immediately expect your superiors to give you direct and conflicting instructions. This is a bad situation. It is imperative that you find out whom you are supposed to listen to when there is a conflict. Make sure that you inform anyone who gives you conflicting instructions that there is a problem. Don't refuse the instructions, just direct them to the other person. Let management struggle over who gets your time.

One common situation occurs when people get "fix-it" type jobs that involve caring for a large variety of equipment in many areas of the organization. At that point, almost anyone may give you an instruction, and all of them will assume you have nothing better to do than their task. The only thing that can save you in this situation is a bureaucracy. There will be more on this in later chapters.

3. Gather All The Office And Technical Equipment That You Can.

You need the works: keys, computers, desks, chairs, lamps, tools, whatever you can get. Often, the first few days on the job are the best opportunity to get handouts of this type. People are always sympathetic to the new person, so take advantage of this rare break and ask for anything you can think of. Maybe you'll even get it.

The general conclusion of this chapter is that you can't afford to go through your first days on a job in a haze. You can't assume that everything will be taken care of, because it probably won't be. You need to make sure that you are able to properly perform your job by taking matters into your own hands. This doesn't mean making yourself difficult or arguing with people, quite the opposite in most cases. What it means is that you should realize that when you join a new organization, you have a limited time to get things working right. You must be proactive, what people like to call a "self-starter".

Chapter Fifteen

The Work Bitching Circle and How to Stay Out of It

"Obstacles are things a person sees when he takes his eyes off his goal."

--- E. Joseph Cossman

What do people do on their lunch hours? Besides eating, I mean. They complain about the boss, right? Or maybe they complain about each other. There is always a lot to complain about. Someone has been moved or transferred and didn't like it. Someone knows of a management decision that wasted money. The smokers don't like the new regulations—and the non-smokers don't like the smokers. Maybe the new hire is a loser, or the lay-offs were unfair.

In particular, there is usually a tight group who makes it their primary mission to complain about everything. They will complain to anyone who will listen. They want new recruits, and when you first start your job, they will try to get you to join them.

Don't do it. In the last chapter I told you to find good mentors to guide you during your first days. I also suggested you establish ties with people to get inside information.

But the complainers are a less useful lot. They might have some good information, but if you hang around with them too much, you will be labeled a complainer. It is this group that will be looked at first when the lay-offs are handed out some day in the future. Hard-core bitching is a sure sign of a demoralized employee that for some reason, right or wrong, is no longer working at their best. Even worse, they tend to spread discord among the others and generally make everyone miserable by endlessly discussing things they have no control of.

People with bad attitudes don't go far in corporate life.

If things are wrong in your organization and you really want to change them, this is the last group that you want to become associated with. No one solves anything by secretly complaining about it. Direct questions posed to management in a very business-like setting are much more effective.

Many people get drawn into ineffective complaining because they feel powerless to change things they see as wrong. Most of these problems have to do with poor management, and there are things you can do to correct them. I will give you some alternatives to endless complaints:

1. Call A Group Meeting, Then Invite Management.

A busy manager will often brush off the worries of a single individual. However, they can rarely resist the urge to join in a larger group discussion. First, gather together your fellow employees with similar complaints. After scheduling a brief time for a meeting on your own, maybe even over lunch so as not to use much company time, invite the appropriate members of management. It is important to announce the meeting, or meetings, and then invite management almost as an afterthought. This way they won't think that they need to orchestrate the gathering.

It is critical that you don't turn this into a roast. If there is someone, present or not, who is at the root of the problem, you don't want to be the one to point any fingers. Everyone else there can figure it out, including the one who is causing the problem.

Sell the meeting as a quick group discussion of a problem area. Write down your complaints in the form of probing questions. The questions should not accuse any individuals by name. They shouldn't accuse anyone of anything directly. Rather, they should point out the problem using careful questions directed at management. Often, the problem is simply unclear or absent instructions from management. This is a very useful way to pin down exactly what it is that they want.

Care should be taken in using this tactic. Arguments frequently break out. If things are going well, these arguments will be between your managers and the result will be some kind of solution to the problem. Things can go badly, however. You might be told to lump it, that there will be no changes.

Abigail, a member of the technical support group at a medium-sized video systems manufacturer that I knew well in the early nineties had serious problems. Her group was responsible for all incoming complaints from customers as well as for keeping all the computers and networking systems in the office building running. This meant that everyone was calling in all hours of the day with problems. If a hard disk crashed in accounting, her department was responsible. If a customer from outside the company called in a complaint about a company product, that was her problem too.

This caused great discord when there were conflicts of resource allocation. If many customer complaints happened to come in simultaneously with the arrival of new company equipment that needed to be installed, she didn't know which to do first. Customers weren't getting their callbacks. Company people were waiting days, even weeks, for new equipment to be delivered that had already come in. The backlog of work seemed endless and heavy.

The worst problem was Abigail's manager, Manuel, the leader of technical support. He wasn't a strong leader, and tended to say yes to anyone who called in with a problem. Anyone could call him personally and get him to say that the problem would be handled "by tomorrow" or "by the end of the week". He would then come to Abigail or one of the others in the group and tell them this was a special circumstance. Regularly, he directed them to drop what they were doing and run to this new crisis.

Of course, that meant that the crisis he had sent them all after last week was dropped. Soon, last week's person would call back and be angry. Then Manuel would unhelpfully accuse his own people of shirking responsibility. After all, he had told them to have that done by yesterday. Never mind that it would take longer and never mind that he had countermanded that order today.

A series of meetings called by Abigail to solve the problem attracted the attention of higher management, who were hearing many complaints by this time. By posing careful questions, for example asking who came first, the customer or the vice president, she illustrated the problem to everyone. Manuel, who had messed up everything by shirking his responsibility to defend his schedule and his people naturally hated the meeting. As one who avoided all conflicts by promising anyone who asked that his underlings would move the moon for them, he was trapped in this situation. His indecision was obvious when put on the spot.

Isolated as the problem, Manuel's department was later broken into two separate entities. He was left in charge only of the internal maintenance support group. A few months later, he was eased out to become a full-time trainer.

Things don't always go this well when you try this tactic. The key is not to make it look like a rebellion, but rather a group of concerned employees looking for solutions.

2. Get Over It.

Much of the time there is nothing you can do about the worst aspects of your job. If the product isn't selling, there is no money and no one is getting a raise this year, so complaints mean nothing.

Try to look at each of the major sore points of your job and see a clean solution. If there isn't one, you might decide to realize there's nothing to be done and take it to heart. Endless complaints about the fact that we can't all breathe water or flap our arms hard enough to fly will do nothing but make everyone around you more miserable.

Teaching at colleges over recent years has provided me with many examples of people bent on this particular folly. As a government-run institution, the cashflow into a college is largely out of the control of the individuals working there. If we do a good job or a bad one, it doesn't make much difference to how much funding we get. This annoys many hardworking people as they feel that constant injustices are being done all around them. If the new stadium gets built, for example, but the teachers' lounge looks like World War II vintage, they see it as a gross injustice. But the fact may well be that one source of money comes from the state and can only be used for new construction. Renovation just didn't get anything this year.

Problems of this nature are just part of the job and shouldn't be allowed to ruin the enjoyment of it. Sometimes seeing and accepting reality can lift the burden from your shoulders.

3. Look For Another Job.

If the problem really eats at you, if you've tried to change it and couldn't, or if you finally realize it's part of the job and you can't accept it, it may be time to move on. In the end, this is one of the prime motivators for switching jobs: disgust with your old job.

Be careful with this attitude, however. If you are a person who is sensitive to injustices, you will be taking that with you to the next place. And believe me, there aren't any niches out there without politics, without greed, without senseless squabbling, without injustice. They just don't exist.

I do encourage you to look, however. There are two possible positive outcomes: you may find something better, or you might not. If you do, take it.

If you don't, maybe your current job won't look so bad to you.

Chapter Sixteen
Stress-Management

"Look at a day when you are supremely satisfied at the end. It's not a day when you lounge around doing nothing; it's when you've had everything to do, and you've done it."

--- Margret Thatcher

Technical work can be very stressful. There are a variety of reasons for this. First, there are the machines. Since you are, by definition, working with equipment, it follows that the equipment won't always perform. The more complex the equipment, the more likely it is to fail. This is simply because there are more things that could possibly go wrong. Think about it this way: Is a house of cards that is built with only ten cards more likely to fall, or one that uses an entire deck? Of course, the larger house is much more likely to collapse. It will fall if any one of those cards is out of place. Therefore, it has 52 chances to fall while the smaller house has only 10 chances for error.

The second reason has to do with our role as fix-it people. When the house of cards finally falls, that's where we, the technical work force, get to come in and pick up the pieces. Worse, we are expected to make the thing work again. Since most technical work arises from problems, technical people hand out a lot of bad news. If you take your car in to get fixed, someone has to tell you how bad it is. Someone must tell you how much it is going to cost. The technical person is then stressed, because the customer is stressed.

I recently took my own Acura into have some work done on it. The bill was over a thousand dollars, and when I came to pick it up, the mechanic was clearly having a hard time telling me. He kept saying, "It's a lot, I'm afraid. A whole lot." Then, before giving me the price, he had to explain every detail of what went wrong. When he finally did tell me, I had pity on the guy and just nodded. I can't say that I smiled, but I didn't complain.

Even then he so expected me to be upset that he began to apologize and rationalize everything. How expensive the parts were, how hard they had worked on the thing, the whole story. I did my best to communicate to him that I wasn't upset, but he seemed stressed anyway.

I found it interesting that he was so defensive, even after having been in the business for more than thirty years. It told me quite a bit about the reactions he was used to getting.

We are in the business of fixing problems and therefore we are in the business of generating stress.

We stress our bosses and ourselves when we tell them the project isn't done yet. We stress everyone when we tell them the idea is a good one, but it probably won't work. We stress people by telling them that this particular widget can't be fixed and that the new one will cost twenty thousand dollars.

Besides the stress of our role of bad news messengers, the very nature of the work is stressful. Many, even most, problems are routine and solvable. But not always. Things that don't work are frustrating. If you are a doctor, and can't fathom what is wrong with a seriously ill patient, that is upsetting. If you can hear the knock in an engine, but after replacing half the parts find that it's still there, you're stressed.

When you work on a computer for months without backing up and your hard disk crashes, you're very disappointed.

Another cause of stress that is inherent in the work is the constant changing of the game. Technology is never still. It never sleeps, not even at night. Even as we sleep, the Chinese are at work. Somewhere out there, perhaps across the globe in Sweden, someone is making a discovery. They are inventing something that you will have to learn about one day. Their discovery will change your life, ever so slightly.

The never-ending learning curve, which I have discussed at length in previous chapters, causes stress. It makes people tense to find that they don't know things, that they have to learn something new.

There is also another, less obvious reason for stress. This stress is caused by the never-ceasing expansion of our burdens. The technical work force is expanding, not contracting. This is particularly true in the area of computers. Everything these days has a computer in it, or a computer was used to make it. Even the service industries, if they have anything to do with information, are being invaded. Nothing is being left unscathed, and the trend is swelling, not slowing down.

If you take a technical job today in a given organization, the role that technology plays in that organization is going to expand. That means that you are going to get more work rather than less. That means that your level of responsibility is going to rise every year.

Many companies that are new to the technology game fail to understand what they are getting into. This is not a new phenomenon.

> *It's a drama that has been played out in industries every year since the first commercial computer system installation at the U. S. Census Bureau in the nineteen fifties.*

When my wife recently made her most recent job-hop, she told me that the company she was going to work for actually believed that her role would dwindle away to nothing with time. They were concerned that after the new system had been put in, she would have nothing to do and would be rather bored. I laughed aloud, and now she does too. Instead of petering out, her job quickly turned into a firestorm. More and more staff has been hired to keep it under control. The system has never worked to perfection, because systems rarely do. And, as soon as they finish some revision level—over-budget and far after completion was scheduled—the next revision looms ahead. Naturally, her position has become pivotal, and the responsibility of it continues to increase.

This has come as a shock to management. Why isn't it all simpler? Can't it all be done in six months and forgotten? All they want to do is get back to business as usual.

Of course, they are in the middle of business as usual; they just don't know it yet because it isn't what they are used to. It is no wonder people have false expectations. They know only what they a salesperson told them. Technology is a whirlwind and once you are in it, everything changes and everything keeps changing. The very nature of everyone's work changes. There is no way out, and no way to avoid it.

If your competitors are on the Internet, for example, they may have an advantage. They may be reaching people that you can't. This is currently killing businesses such as real estate listing services: If you can find a million homes for sale on the net with video walk-throughs and cross-indexed pricing, who needs a paper-based service?

The point is that virtually every organization has to grow and change. There is no sitting still. There is no avoiding computers by refusing to buy them. If nothing else, customers will begin to shun you for not being "with it". Everyone is getting into the technology game, and once in, they will be continuously pulled deeper into the storm.

This is both good and bad for us. It ensures that we, the "techies", will bring home bacon and have good career opportunities. But like the old Chinese curse, *may you live in interesting times*, we will find ourselves regularly stressed. The very expansion of our work year by year means that we will never be caught up, and almost always be overworked and understaffed.

Okay, so we have thoroughly covered all the reasons why our work is stressful. Fine. But what do we do about it? If you can't really get rid of these causes, how do you cope with them?

1. Learn To Accept The Stressful Nature Of The Job.

Acceptance is a critical first step. Realize that you are never going to get to the bottom of the list, because by the time you are halfway down it will have doubled in size. Your goal should never be to complete all your work. Rather, you should view it as a continuum. Think of your work as a pipeline, where things come in, get set with a priority, then eventually filter their way down to getting done. The key is to focus on one thing at a time and get it finished. Often, even this seems impossible.

But remember, you don't really ever want to finish all your work. Then you'd be out of a job! Fortunately, this will probably never happen. Technical work is like a bowl of cracked wheat; it keeps growing, even as you eat it.

2. Learn To Cope With Frustration.

Technical work isn't clean. Usually you can't just "do it" and ship it out, and hope it isn't too bad. You've got to do more than that; you have to do it *right*. You have to make something *work*.

Machines and systems that don't work can be incredibly frustrating at times. If you are infuriated with puzzles, you need to get over it—fast.

3. Learn How To Deliver Bad News.

Part of every technical person's work is the delivery of bad tidings. Like every doctor, you need to work on your bedside manner. Be sensitive to your clients and management. Don't lie, and don't make excuses. Instead, become an expert at rationalizations and looking at the bright side of things.

4. Learn How To Estimate Project Time And Money.

One of the keys to this is being a bit pessimistic at the outset of any project. Don't tell them it can't be done, not unless you really think it can't, but do make sure you are estimating enough time and money to do it right, plus some padding.

If you listen to upper management and salespeople, mountains can be moved in "two weeks", or "by the end of the year." The technical people know better. One of the hardest things people have to do in technical work is estimate the time and money it will take to get a job done. In general, money isn't as hard to figure out as time. One of the reasons that time is so hard to calculate is there are almost always going to be interruptions. Often, it is difficult even to get to a small project, as constant crises come up that demand your attention.

Unfortunately, people outside your group will tend to figure out how much time the job should take and then promise it will be done by then. Of course, you are probably doing six other things at the same time, some of which you haven't even heard about yet.

A colleague named Kurt gave a simple formula to me. He was a self-made millionaire in the computer software industry. He told me to always make my best guess, either in weeks, months or years, then double it and add three. Therefore, if you think it will take six weeks, tell them fifteen.

It sounded crazy, but it worked for me for years. He explained it this way: everything takes twice as long as you think it will. The plus three gives you some extra padding and keeps the number from sounding too even. If you say six weeks or six months, it sounds like you are taking a stab. If you say fifteen weeks, it sounds like you really know what you are talking about. It makes the number sound very well thought-out.

There is another critical point here. People hate it when you tell them a time and can't stick to it. Let's say you have a project and you say it will take six weeks, but it takes ten. Now everyone is angry because you are late. But, if you said fifteen and it takes ten, you look like a wizard because you got it done so fast. Same project, same amount of time, but with different expectations set for people.

5. Educate Everyone You Can.

In the end, one of the keys roles of technical people is to educate everyone we can so that they can do their jobs properly. Not everyone is interested, but teach whomever you can anyway. Don't try to force the secretaries to learn how to change the toner cartridge if they resist, but find one who will do it. People will respond much better to seeing others get ahead of them than they will to your best direct urgings.

Your workload is going to be overwhelming, so recruit help wherever you can. In many cases the best person to solve a technical problem is the person who discovers it.

There is a popular story, billed as a genuine account, which floats about on the Internet. It concerns uneducated users and it goes something like this:

The beleaguered technical support person answers the phone:

> *"Hello, I'm your customer and I recently purchased one of your systems. Now I'm having a problem with it."*
>
> *"And what's that, sir?"*
>
> *"The cup-holder broke,"* said the customer a bit accusingly. *"I can see that it was never properly built in the first place. It isn't very strong plastic."*
>
> *"Cup-holder?"* asked the baffled support person. *"But sir, our systems don't come with cup-holders. Is this something that you've added?"*
>
> *"No, it was there when I first purchased the computer. It's always been there. I just push the button and—"*

> *At that point, the technical support person put the customer on hold and hung her head in defeat. She just couldn't stand it. The user had been using the DVD drive as a cup-holder and had broken it.*
>
> *I use this example, because true or not, this sort of thing happens all the time. The only way out of it is to educate the ignorant. In the end, it saves us all a lot of time, energy—and cup-holders.*

6. Build A Bureaucracy To Defend Yourself.

In general, I'm not a believer in bureaucracies. There are times, however, when they are indispensable. If you are in the position of providing technical assistance to a large group of people, a bureaucracy is a must. In almost every case, your workload is going to increase steadily over time. This means you will soon be overloaded, if you aren't already. Many new organizations start with a single individual who is responsible for a wide variety of tasks. Using the tried and true approach of management, they won't fix something until it breaks. The individual providing the support is often the piece that quits or complains effectively enough to get more help.

At this point the expansion of the support department is on, and no matter what kind of technical service you are providing, it will continue to grow.

Being bombarded with requests makes it difficult to get things done. What you need is a simple system that identifies tasks, prioritizes them and assigns them to individual people.

If you were the one to manage such a thing, as I have done in the past, I would recommend that you don't put too many tasks on any one person. When a new task comes in, put it in the queue, but don't assign it right away. If a person has just two or three tasks waiting, they will feel better and more in control than if they have twenty work orders over their heads. If your people know what they are to do for the rest of the week and perhaps have an inkling about next week, that is good enough. As management, it is your job to worry about what is to be done with the rest of the list.

Also, try never to change their short list. If you keep it short for each individual, you can change next week's plan without them feeling as if you are pulling the rug out from under them. This is because next week's plan hasn't even been revealed to them yet. People hate having the tasks they are to do switched frequently. Give them the illusion of steady progress and they will work more effectively.

7. Don't Work Yourself To Death.

This may seem obvious, but it isn't always when you are in the heat of battle. There are times when we all become convinced that if we just worked twelve or more hours a day we could get things done. This might be true in some occupations, at least for a short while. But it is counterproductive in technical work because you need your whole brain to function. If you are tired, you can often take hours to do a task that would take just minutes if you were sharp and well rested. Getting stubborn and pounding away at something can work, up to a point. Staying an extra hour or two once a week tends to get things done. Studies have shown that working more than ten hours a day, however, is a losing strategy. This is especially true for mental work. Even eight hours can be too long for our weary minds. At the end of the day your effectiveness will drop and you won't be able to see the answer anymore.

As part of pacing yourself, you need to remember the basics of life at all times. You need to eat. Drink fluids to keep yourself awake. You need to take breaks, even if just to walk around the building and think. You need to get exercise whenever you can. Your primary asset is your brain, and keeping it functioning at top efficiency is your goal. Why spend ten extra hours or days on a project that you could have done in half the time if you were at your best?

8. Make Lists And Tick Things Off Of Them.

Lists not only force you to focus on what you are doing, they can be satisfying to both you and management. Every day, or at least once a week, you should make a list of what you want to get accomplished in that time span. If your projects are very large, write down some small steps you are working on.

Put as many things on your list as you can. Put down things that you've already accomplished today, so that the whole list isn't depressingly incomplete. One item on all of my lists is: "make today's list". This sounds silly, but it gets you into the mode of completing things.

Another critical advantage of working by lists is that when management asks the question: "What have you done for us lately?" you always have a ready answer. Sometimes, this is worth a raise or even your job.

9. Set Aside Time To Do "The Big Project".

Many of us in technical work have more to do than just the day-to-day. We are tasked to work on several things at once, such as maintaining a hundred machines, supporting a hundred people and making the next Big Upgrade happen. This can be maddening, as the same people who chide you in meetings for not finishing the "big project" will turn around the same day and ask you to drop everything for their pet problem.

The only way around this situation is to divide your day. It would be nice to simply stop the day-to-day and not do it, but that is unrealistic. The best way to divide your day is into halves. With lunch as the break point, work either mornings or afternoons on the "big project" and do your regular support the rest of the time.

Of course, you need management approval to do this. Normally, this isn't too hard to get, if they really want you to finish the big project. The trick isn't getting approval, but keeping it. As soon as your voicemail begins to pile up and the complaints start to roll in about slow service, they will start wanting you to do everything at once again, which is impossible, but sounds nice.

Your real goal in this type of situation is to get more staff to do your old work. This is the only real way you will get the time to do "the big project". Your job is to make management realize this.

Chapter Seventeen
How NOT to Make Enemies

"There are two kinds of people, those who work and those who take the credit. Try to be in the first group; there is less competition there."

--- Indira Gandhi

One of the surest ways to keep your job is to make friends. Even if you aren't very good at your job, you can hold on to it if you are likable. In most employment situations, you will start off with a friendly greeting from everyone. By just paying a bit of attention to everyone you meet, you will quickly find yourself surrounded by friends. They might not go to bat for you, but they aren't out to knife you in a meeting, either.

When things get tough in the company, the decision of whom to fire usually won't be made on the basis of merit. If everyone hates you, or even just a few key people do, you will be tossed overboard. And the crew will sail away, cheering your demise.

So why is it that we tend to gather enemies? Here are some things to avoid:

1. Avoid Sexual And Emotional Relationships In The Workplace.

I know it can be hard to find someone when you are busy and never get out. I'm guilty myself of dating people from work. It's easy to do. They are always around, easy to talk to and often have related interests. There is never a lack of something to say because you can always talk about work.

But when things go wrong, it can be hell. All too often, you have an instant enemy on your hands when the relationship ends. Others, too, will resent the relationship. What if you or your partner gets jealous? Suddenly, more enemies abound.

2. Realize That When You Oppose Something, You Are Upsetting The People Who Are Backing It.

Whenever you publicly attack an idea in which others have an interest, you might be making enemies. This happened to me on more than one occasion. When I was working as the V.P. of Software Development, I felt I had to argue against using a programming language that I thought had little commercial future. For several years, I frequently discussed changing that language. I finally did succeed and everyone agreed it was for the better, but during those years I unwittingly had gained an enemy. The man heading up the language support group must have always felt attacked by my arguments.

This enemy, who I had helped to get hired and had once counted as a friend, over time came to cost me dearly. It was a strain to have someone who was always sour and unforgiving at every gathering. I made some attempts to mend fences, but by then he had come up with a dozen other reasons to dislike me, and nothing worked.

The odd thing about it was that by the end of our struggle we both agreed that the right decision had been made about the programming language, but that didn't matter. I had made the enemy anyway. Being right didn't make things any better. Perhaps they even made it worse.

3. Never Belittle People.

If someone says something foolish, don't patronize them. Always treat people as adults, even if they don't act like adults. People become unglued if you insinuate they don't know what they are talking about, especially if they don't. If they think you consider their ideas laughable, they will hate you. You don't want *anyone* to hate you.

4. In Arguments, Never Get Personal, Even If They Do.

Try to stay mature at all times. Try not to shout, and above all don't respond to personal attacks. Often when people are losing arguments and getting angry, they lash out with personal remarks. Your goal should be to get them back to the point of the argument. If you can ignore their personal attacks long enough, people will usually snap out of their immature behavior and respond to your professional even-tempered manner. They may even start to feel foolish and apologize. At that point, some serious communication can begin.

It's okay to attack someone's idea, if you must. But you can never call them a fat slob. Even if they are a fat slob, and they are calling you a four-eyed, snot-nosed kid, it doesn't help to get personal. At that point, you are just angry at each other and nothing is getting resolved.

Actually, that isn't true. What is happening is far worse: the two of you are cementing a relationship of anger and mistrust. You are making a personal enemy of that person, and that is simply unwise.

5. If You Are The Boss, It Is Easy To Make Enemies.

They are called your employees. No one has the power to make enemies like a boss. Many people harbor a touch of resentment towards authority figures. This magnifies very quickly if they feel that you have abused your power over them.

When you are the boss, your people must see you in a positive light. As a manager, the very nature of your job is to manage, that is to get a job done properly using the talents of others. People who dislike you won't get the job done properly. They won't back you up when you need them.

The chief way that you can gain their trust, loyalty and instant support is by being on their side. You should do whatever you can to protect your employees from other managers, etc. You should take their side in every argument, not use them as scapegoats. This approach works well with most people.

6. If You Do Well, Don't Brag Too Much About It.

People automatically dislike braggarts. I'm not talking about calmly pointing out at your employee review that you finished your project two weeks early and you always get to work on time, that's normal and expected. I'm talking about bragging. The more you tell people how great you are, the less they will think of you in most cases. You can be sure that the people around you are very aware of how good you are. If you are the best, everyone will know it. If you are quiet enough about it, they might even like you instead of hating you for it.

I worked with a salesman who regularly grossed the most money each month. Every month Bert would take the sales chart, blow it up on the copy machine and hang it up on his office door. His top earnings would be circled in thick, blood-red felt pen. Three or four exclamation marks would make sure you couldn't miss his swollen number. Even worse, Bert would sometimes also circle another salesperson's total that was unusually low and put a big question mark beside it.

I've never met a man more hated by his peers. When a pack of salespeople turn on you, things can go very badly. The very power of persuasion that they possess can be turned into a force of evil under such circumstances. To make a long story short, they worked hard to switch his territory to one that didn't pay, then told many lies to management as to why he couldn't make the old numbers that he used to. I believe they may even have arranged a few embarrassments with customers for him. After a few bad quarters, he became demoralized and was laid off.

7. Don't Be A Phony.

If you don't know what people are talking about, don't act like you do. This is similar to bragging and it often shows an inner lack of self-confidence. Even if it doesn't, people will take it that way.

Remember: *in technical work, no one knows everything*. As things continue to change and the rate of change increases, people aren't expected to know it all. Even if you do know it all, it's only good for a few months, and then there is a lot of new stuff to learn.

Sometimes, in an interview or a sales situation particularly, you might have to smile and nod and let them assume you understand what they are talking about. Otherwise your all-knowing facade will fail. Then, on the first break you get, you run off and try to figure it out.

Even this is dangerous, however. In most cases, it is far better to stop them and ask a few intelligent questions. Most people will respect you more for this.

8. Expect Enemies To Appear In Competitive Situations.

Competition between people can be an excellent motivator. It can also breed a nest of vipers. Salespeople who are working on a competitive basis frequently fall into this trap. Even though the job of a salesperson is officially to make friends, they seem to make enemies of one another quite easily.

One older salesman once told me that every good salesman carried a stiletto up his sleeve—just in case.

"What about saleswomen?" I asked him.

"Oh, they don't bother with knives," he told me. "They carry guns."

10. Don't Always Take The Credit.

We often forget in our enthusiasm that enemies can be made when things seem to be going very well. One of the fastest ways to gain enemies is to claim someone else's work as your own. Even if you did most of the work, make sure you mention them, and not just in passing. Make a clear statement indicating who helped you—and do it in public, preferably in front of the boss. Everyone will think more of you for it. If you need to clarify that you were the main force behind the success, do it in private, or let someone else say it.

Dealing With Enemies

In time, most people will find they have an enemy or two to be dealt with. If you strictly avoided the above situations, how did you get them? Sometimes, the process is inevitable. Perhaps the other person's personality clashes with yours. Perhaps you are in direct competition of some kind and therefore your gain is the other's loss.

So if you have enemies, how do you handle them?

1. Sue For Peace.

If you realize that someone is your enemy, consider asking them for peace. Start off by saying: "I know we aren't getting along terribly well. What can I do to change that?"

This offer might be rejected, or the person might deny there is a problem, but it will usually shock them. Sometimes confronting the person about the situation can do wonders. In my experience a person who does this is rare indeed, although it seems like an obvious move. If the person is afraid to publicly acknowledge their animosity towards you they might back off when they are faced with the truth.

2. Confront Them On The Issues.

Some of the worst enemies are those that smile at your face while stabbing your back. At all costs find out who is against you and confront them about it. This works particularly well with people who like to operate behind the scenes by complaining to your boss and co-workers. People like this will often do anything they can to avoid a direct confrontation. If you do confront them about it, they might back off.

I maintain a policy that has helped for many years to keep an uneasy truce between myself and others that want to have a turf-war with me. (And believe me, there are people like this everywhere.) The policy goes something like this: If someone tells my boss something negative about me, rather than telling me directly, I will immediately contact them and ask them about it. I will try to discuss it calmly and at length. I will try to elicit from them a promise not to repeat the mistake of bypassing me again the next time they have a problem with my performance.

The conflict might be anything, a fight over money, office space, personnel, management structure. It doesn't matter what it is about, what matters is the procedure for resolving it. I've frequently found that people who run to complain to your supervisor while still smiling at you are cowardly. They will usually back down if you show them that you will turn the situation into a confrontation, which is exactly what they don't want. Next time they will think twice before being a tattletale.

3. Sometimes You Have To Fight.

If you do have an enemy and you can't make them happy and you can't back them off, it is often a good idea to separate the two of you. This can be done in many ways besides murder, of course. You might try to get one of you transferred so that you'll be out of each other's way. You could try to get them promoted or even try to get them another job. That way they will be out of your hair. They might even start liking you for doing them a favor.

Unless the enemy is working for you, I don't suggest that you try to get them fired. This sort of thing is dangerous, and stresses the rest of the staff as they are often asked to take up sides. Transfers or new jobs are usually positive and far more acceptable to everyone than termination.

I worked hard to transfer one enemy from our West Coast office to our East Coast office. I managed it, and even though it only lasted for two years, it was blissful. Another enemy I actually found a new job for outside of the company. Today, oddly enough, we consider each other friends.

These tactics can backfire on you if management discovers them and isn't pleased. I recommend them only if you are desperate. You don't want to be labeled a schemer—especially if you are one sometimes.

Chapter Eighteen

Travel, Opportunity and Your Family

"May you live in interesting times."

--- Ancient Chinese Curse

One of the age-old truths of career-building is that the more successful you are the more your family life suffers. By successful, I mean the higher you advance in an organization.

It happens to many of us: We climb by way of the corporate ladder, or perhaps by opportunistic job-hopping. Each year we bring home a fatter check, but seem to spend less time with the spouse and children. There is less time for exercise and social events too, which tends to alter our personalities. The fun-loving sort that our spouses married ten years ago is gone. We become company people, truly living for our jobs, rather than our families. At this point, divorce and problems with our kids begin to plague us.

What should we do? Should we fear success? Is advancement in an organization a proud moment or a death-knell for our families?

No, we shouldn't fear success, but we must always weigh in the damage done to our personal lives by each step we take in our careers. We should always consider, when pondering a new job, what does this mean to my family?

Danger Signs

1. Stressful Working Conditions.

Stress at your work will leak into your family life. You can control it to some extent, but not always. People who are dead-tired and in a bad mood every night don't make good parents or spouses. The important thing here is to realize that you will take home part of your job with you. Even if you don't want to, you won't always be able to shield your family from your work.

2. Long Hours.

Don't count just the hours you are going to be at work. Count in the time it takes to get ready, commute, eat lunch and do extra work that you might take home with you. How many waking hours a day are left for your family? How many hours are there before your kids are asleep?

Your family doesn't just need quality time, they need *time*. Lots of it. In my book, doing just about anything with them works wonders. Even the mere fact of your presence will affect everything. Do you want be able to trust your spouse and make sure your kids aren't sneaking home with illegal substances in plastic baggies? Then *be there*.

One way that I've seen people balance a heavy workload with family life is to take some of it home with them. I do this now myself with practically all my preparations and grading. I bring everything I can home from the college. When I do software development or I'm working on a book, I do it at home. It might take me twice as long to do it all with my family roaming around and asking for things, but at least I'm home and I know what's going on there. I know this is the opposite of advice you may often get where better work performance is the goal. But in my life, that isn't the only goal. Besides, if your family is suffering, believe me, your work will suffer too. The point is to strike a balance and to try to keep it.

2. Travel.

Job transfers to other states or even other countries are frequently prerequisites to career-climbing. Surprisingly, I've found that these sorts of things are less damaging to family life than one might think. Sure, everyone misses the old house, school and neighborhood. Perhaps your relatives aren't as close anymore. But this very isolation can pull a family together. Since you are the only familiar people in a new environment, your dependency upon one another increases.

Travel is only dangerous when you *don't* take your family with you. How much time apart a family can take varies, but it seems to cause problems for most people once it becomes more than one short trip a month, or if the trips last longer than two weeks. This isn't true of all families. Many survive or even thrive despite lengthy and frequent separations. In my experience, however, these families are the exception rather than the rule.

I've done a lot of traveling. I've cashed in frequent flier miles for new tickets nine times, and that was only for the airlines I bothered to keep track with. In one eight-year period, I went on more than one hundred out-of-state business trips lasting anywhere from one day to six weeks. I've worked in nine countries, including Mexico, Belgium, Finland and Russia.

This may all sound exciting—and at times it is—but it can get old quickly. I recall one lazy spring afternoon that started with me munching on a brown bag lunch and clicking at the keyboard on my desk. After a few stormy phone calls, I found myself in Calgary, Canada by dinnertime. On another occasion, Thanksgiving dinner was interrupted with the news that I would be leaving the following day to spend the rest of the holiday season in Paris.

For nearly a decade, I never really unpacked. All of my toiletry things were in a shaving kit, ready to go. I used the shaving kit every day, whether I was at home or not, without even thinking about it. My clothes weren't permanently in suitcases, but the matching row of well-beaten maroon Samsonite veterans were always ready for instant action in the hall closet. My briefcase was never without the traveling necessities: passport, extra credit card and cash, phone card, an assortment of over-the-counter drugs and a package of crackers for those time-change midnight hunger pains.

Which brings us to the special stresses of travel: Jet-lag is a subtle thing, sometimes vicious, sometimes just a surreal feeling. One time I'll get off the plane in Prague or Barcelona and within a day I'll feel fine. At other times I simply can't seem to adjust, falling asleep on the job at 4:00 P.M. and wide awake watching crappy TV at 3:00 A.M. Getting your body not to be hungry at night and not to be sleepy in the day can be murder. What's worse, adjusting on the way back is another ordeal. The only tip I have is to force yourself to maintain the new schedule, whatever it is, and stay up later rather than try to sleep earlier. If you can skip a whole night of sleep, you will crash the next night and—if you are lucky—awaken refreshed and adjusted.

Remember, if there is a time change even of four or five hours, don't make any important decisions the next day. Try not to work at all, but if you have to, keep it as light as possible until you adjust. I've seen people who could adjust very easily ten times, but then couldn't on the eleventh. You never know when jet-lag is going to get you.

The point of all this is to demonstrate to you that travel is a strain on the traveler. When you return from a trip, even an easy one, you will be tired. Sometimes you will be utterly exhausted. Your family will want to go out and have a big meal at a restaurant, while you will want nothing more than a home-cooked meal. They will want to go to the park with you, while you will want to soak your feet.

If you are young and have no family, travel may make life interesting. But once other people start to depend on you to be around, frequent or long absences become a problem.

Even when you're single there are problems. Pets are hard to keep alive. I myself must have murdered two dozen houseplants through sheer neglect. Weird things may happen at home while you're gone. One time I came back from a month in England to discover than my home alarm system had been dismantled from the outside. Rushing into the house in a panic, I discovered nothing missing. My neighbors later explained that they had disconnected the thing because it had been going off randomly every day for a week. I searched the house for the cause and finally figured it out: A large spider had taken up residence directly over the motion-detector in the living room. Whenever this beast decided to travel his web, he set off the alarm. I wonder now if the noise bothered him.

Final Note on Career vs. Family

I've listed three major things to look out for that tend to stress your family: stress at work, long hours and travel. *"But wait!"* you say, *"Aren't those just the sort of things that people must do to get ahead?"*

Exactly. Climbing the career ladder requires sacrifice. You must carefully judge just how much you are willing to give up to advance in your career.

Always remember that your job might not be there tomorrow.

The only people who will mourn it with you and help you get your next one are the very people you are ignoring to excel at it. Don't get me wrong, I believe in doing your best, working hard and getting ahead. I want swimming pools, big houses and fast cars as much as the next guy. But I always like to know what I'm giving up for it.

No job is worth risking my family.

Chapter Nineteen
How to Manage Techies

"The mind is like a TV set—when it goes blank, it's a good idea to turn off the sound."

--- *Communication Briefings*

This chapter is aimed at anyone who has the job of managing a group of technical professionals. If you are a technical worker who has had the dedication it takes to rise up into management or to become the owner of a growing firm, this chapter is written for you.

Even if you aren't in management now, perhaps you will be in the future. The shift into management for technical people can come early and suddenly. Moving into management from technical work can be a shock. It is an extremely different job. Instead of emphasizing equipment and technical knowledge, people and their problems are the main issue. If you are successful in a technical field, you may someday be offered a management position. Beware that the knowledge that has made you a success up until now won't be enough. Technical expertise can't guide a team of people on a project. You need people skills as well.

There are racks of books written on management techniques, ethics and style. I won't repeat here what has already been said elsewhere. This chapter is focused on dealing with issues that are unique to technical management.

I will argue with anyone that managing technical people is an art apart from traditional management.

Technical people are usually bright and motivated (although not always in the direction you wish them to be). They tend to be hard workers. Despite these positive factors, they can be difficult to deal with.

"It's kind of like herding cats," joked a colleague of mine after an unsuccessful meeting with his staff. It seemed that everyone had their own ideas as to how to design a project, and since none of them were clearly superior or inferior, chaos had resulted.

Technical people are creative and easily bored by repetition. They can be very dedicated workers, but tend to have social problems at work or at home.

I have compiled here a list of "problem" personality profiles that I have encountered repeatedly. Along with these profiles are suggested ways to handle each of them.

1. **The Maverick.**

This individual is hard-working, capable—and perhaps just a bit arrogant about it. They do very well on smaller, one-person jobs. Unfortunately, they seem to know nothing of teamwork.

If they work in a team, they view the others as competitors rather than comrades. They want the credit for everything and like to show-off whenever possible. The difficulty with this type of person is that they can't function well on larger projects, not because they lack the technical know-how, but rather because they lack the ability to function as part of a group.

This type of individual (and I would have to count myself as one of them in my early career) is very common in this country. We train our people with the western traditions of individuality and personal competition. Good technical people come from a background of being the best at something. They are used to that status and wish to keep it.

If you want to get the most out of a successful Maverick, then make him or her into a project leader. If they are running a group, and have responsibility for the project, they will do well. Dealing with others will teach them a lot. They may even learn how to work as part of a team that someone else is running on the next project.

2. The Pontificator.

This is a more harmless variety of technical person who loves to talk to anyone and everyone about their work. They truly love the sound of their own voice and love nothing more than to blow on for ten minutes or more at meetings, whether or not they have anything useful to say. They tend to annoy the other workers with their speeches, which are often very boastful and sometimes even absurd.

Underneath, this is usually a very insecure person. They are trying to impress everyone with their knowledge and accomplishments, and honestly don't realize that everyone else is rolling their eyes at them. That doesn't mean that they aren't good workers, or that they don't like their jobs. They just have a habit of making their annoying speeches.

This sort of person shouldn't be allowed into management in any form. If you have ever had a boss like this, you'll what I mean. I generally don't confront them about their poor social skills, as they tend to be too fragile to take any sort of personal criticism. Rather, they need a manager who will gently guide them back into their spot when necessary. I've dealt with quite a few personalities of this type successfully. At a meeting, for example, I always let them have their moment in the limelight. I check the clock when they start and I let them blow on for five to ten minutes. By that time everyone there is fidgeting and dying for relief. Often, even the pontificator is running out of gas, but still drones on. I will then intercede with a smile and a quick—but very firm—thanks for the input. Often, they will try to keep going, but I simply talk over them, more loudly—without pausing to give them another chance. I talk directly to the others, not to the problem individual. After the pontificator sees that I have everyone else's attention, silence will usually prevail.

If you really need to discuss something with someone like this, get him or her alone in your office or theirs and discuss it privately. The more other people there are around you the more they will tend to chatter. Oftentimes, this type can be very normal when speaking to you alone, but nearly out-of-control in a group.

3. The Slob.

This is a person who has poor personal hygiene. Their work areas tend to be a disorganized mess. They eat at their desks and never clean up anything.

Now, I want it to be clear that the type of Slob I'm talking about isn't just a young bachelor who doesn't always shave or wear a fresh shirt. I'm talking about a real problem character. An individual that only seems to wash for interviews—if then.

The Slob is usually a combination character. He or she (yes, I've worked with more than one female Slob) will often have other unpleasant quirks as well. Rarely is someone a true Slob and yet a completely functional worker in every other respect. I've worked with a variety of people like this and have rarely been satisfied with their results.

Don't get me wrong: I'm not someone who can't overlook personal habits if the worker is good enough. It's just that in my experience, these individuals are a pain to work with. Their poor habits almost always are an outward display of hostility towards authority figures.

As their manager, this simply means: *they don't like you.* It is hard to get good work out of someone who, underneath it all, truly doesn't like or trust you. You can try to make friends with them, but they will always be looking for your true, dark nature. So as soon as you tell them something they don't like, you are the enemy again, and all your efforts have been wasted.

Of the people I've personally fired, at least half I would consider to be Slobs. I didn't fire them for their personal habits—where others might have—but for other reasons.

4. The "Details" Fanatic.

This bulldog of a character will tend to fixate upon a few technical details and refuse to let go. It is very difficult to have a high-level planning discussion with them, as they can't keep their minds from trying to work out every technical detail on the spot. This is a more rare type, but I've encountered a fair number in my career. Often, they demonstrate qualities similar to the pontificator, but their goals aren't the same. They aren't necessarily insecure, but rather have an uncontrollable urge to understand microscopic details about any suggested project.

This type of person tends to be very competent, but is difficult to talk to. They tend to be a bit nervous and excitable when technical issues are discussed. In fact, they often can make it impossible to have a general planning-level meeting.

It is best to limit their input during meetings. One method I use to do this is by excusing them from meetings early to do other work, etc. Always give them a specific task to do. You could, for example, talk to them before the meeting and say:

"I need you to present your plans for ten minutes, tops. Then you can get out of there while the others chew it over. The discussion would only waste your valuable time."

5. The Mannequin.

This person might well be a technical wizard, but when you talk to them, you start to wonder if they could fog a mirror. They seem all but lifeless, devoid of personality and opinion. Noncommittal grunts and nods are oftentimes all I can get from these individuals.

The shy-type is fairly common. There must be at least one for every Pontificator, perhaps just to even life out. They aren't as noticeable, of course, because they are quiet. Sometimes, these people make very good workers. They tend to get more done while the rest of us are talking.

I believe the key with these people is to leave them alone. Making it your project to "bring them out of their shell" is rarely fruitful or worth the effort. If they want to change, they will do it themselves. If you can get them into a spot where communication with other humans is rarely required, they can often do well. Naturally, they aren't management material.

A word of caution, however: If a person like this is harboring a bad-attitude or some other negative characteristic, it can be much harder for you to detect and deal with. I've been taken by surprise by Mannequins who had other problems that I couldn't detect for a long time due to their quiet natures.

6. The Tinkering Packrat.

This is another common variety of individual. This person really works for you so that they can play with the equipment and collect more of it. They love new machines, the more cosmetic the better. They seem to just like to stack equipment up, higher and higher, whether they need it or not. Each new item that they talk you into budgeting fascinates them for only so long, and then they are on to the next toy.

I happen to like Tinkering Packrats, but they can be troubling. On the good side, they tend to be very knowledgeable, and by definition they keep up with the latest technology in their fields. On the bad side, they often have difficulty finishing projects as they are easily bored and want to be off to the next toy. They also tend to cost you a lot, always insisting that they need the latest and greatest equipment, no matter what the price.

These people are best used as sources of information. They are good at technical support and maintenance. They are usually congenial and can be very good at getting new things to work. They can sometimes make good trainers, but rarely have the patience or people skills required for sales work.

7. The Bad-Attitude Type.

This individual often comes from a large company or governmental background. They see their job as just labor they are forced to deal with in order to eat. Management is a dark enemy, and co-workers are suspected spies. Every change is viewed in a personally negative light: If offices are switched around, it is seen as some type of demotion. If new people are hired, management is wasting money on idiots when existing staff could do the work. If people are laid-off, management is driving the place to bankruptcy and exercising personal vendettas against the naysayers.

The Bad-Attitude types are always part of the work bitching-circle. They spend much of lunch complaining about the boss—as long as the boss isn't around. And sometimes even if the boss is present.

This type is hard to deal with. In some cases, I try to work around their mistrustful exterior—or even ignore it—if I can get useful work out of them. The problem is that you are always paying a price to have this person on your staff. They are bringing down the others, even if it isn't obvious. This person needs to change their attitude on their own, and maybe a direct confrontation with them about it will help. Sometimes, people have told me that they didn't know the others thought of them as a big complainer. They were honestly surprised, and I managed to shock them out of it by simply bringing it to their attention.

As a rule, I try not to hire this type of person, and if I accidentally do, I try to alter their behavior or get rid of them as soon as I can.

8. The Savior.

This person can't say no. You might assign them, very explicitly, to a certain task. You might give them a time for completion, a written workorder, etc. But as soon as you walk out the door, if anyone else asks for something, they drop your project and run to do the new task.

Of course, once people realize they've got someone jumping to their call, soon everyone is in on the bonanza of service. Channels are ignored and private deals are made. In the end, every project in the organization is getting done but yours. Soon, they are over-committed to everyone and can't get anything done. The Savior is going home exhausted and overworked, but still isn't succeeding.

This individual needs protection. When dealing with them, try to remember that are just trying to help everyone. The real culprits are those who are capitalizing on your weak link. It is hard to keep them from over-doing it, however, so I suggest giving the Savior a bureaucratic system of paperwork that can't be deviated from. You must give them, and everyone else, a very clear channel to the Savior's services. Then fight to strictly maintain it.

Is Everyone an Oddball?

The first question I usually get from someone reading this chapter is: Why? Why are there so many people with odd personalities in these fields? Why do you techies behave so oddly?

Reviewing these eight personality profiles, I see facets of myself in all of them. I suppose this gives me some grounds to answer the question.

First of all, we techies are usually bright people. That makes a lot of us a bit eccentric to begin with. Secondly, working with equipment and concepts isn't like working with people. The skills you gain in this kind of work aren't the same ones that most people develop in other jobs.

Since this book is really written for us—the "techies"—I will conclude by suggesting that all of us try to avoid these profiles. There are times when any of us might fall into these behavioral traps. It is important for all of us to realize how others see us and remember that our people skills are at least as important to our success as is our technical expertise.

Chapter Twenty
Take-Overs and Lay-Offs

"A man can succeed at almost anything for which he has unlimited enthusiasm."

--- Charles M. Schwab

These days everyone seems to be "down-sizing" or "acquiring new subsidiaries". Both of these terms usually spell doom for a goodly number of employees. Downsizing means laying off as many people as you can, often entire departments. The biggest cost of most companies is in paying their employees. If they want to look profitable for any reason, even if the boost will only last for a short time, they frequently decide to trim back staff.

Very recently, as of this writing, there was a lay-off at my wife's company. I specifically asked her to investigate the affair as research for this book. This is her description:

Monday morning, just before lunch, a select group of people was asked to report to the Personnel Director's office. There they were informed that they were all being laid off, effective immediately. It was an utter surprise to all of them. Some had been working with the company for ten years or more. One of the women was pregnant at the time.

They were each handed folders with their termination papers in them. They were asked for their keys and security cards, which were laid on the Personnel Director's desk. Their things would be boxed and sent to them, they were informed. They were then collectively escorted to the door and put aboard the express elevator going down to the building's lobby.

The day had begun as any other for them. They had all been calmly working at their desks, considering what they would do for their lunch hours. Fifteen minutes later they found themselves on the street at midday. They were bewildered and no longer employed. Their lunch hour had been extended indefinitely.

This cold approach to handling terminations is more common each year. I attribute this primarily to the increase of lawsuits on the part of disgruntled employees. Additionally, there seems to be an increasing level of fear on the part of management concerning terminated employees. They worry about sabotage and theft. "Two weeks notice" seems only to apply to people who are quitting, and isn't a consideration when people are being terminated.

Take-Overs

When two companies merge into one, it usually happens because one bought out the stock of another. Employees who are caught in the middle when two mountainous organizations crash together are often crushed. Take-overs are always uncomfortable and sometimes downright frightening.

I've seen take-overs from both angles. I've been in a team of people that reviews another organization before or after a take-over. This is uncomfortable for both sides. Often, you are instructed not to tell any of the employees of either company what is going on. Why? Because management is afraid people will panic and try to protect themselves by hiding information or stealing files from computers, etc. This means that you will often appear unannounced—like gray-suited government agents. I indeed, have felt like some kind of thug, expressionlessly shoving people away from their desks and digging through their work. I didn't enjoy the experience any more than they did.

I've been on the other side, too, when the unsmiling strangers appear. The effect on your co-workers is electric. Fear and shock register on everybody's face as they realize that they might not have a job when the sun next rises. It's a grim moment, let me tell you.

I personally don't think this sort of approach is smart, but these days the tension between management and their employees is high. By day, they all seem comfortable with one another, but it takes just a few changes at the top for all pretense of civilized behavior to drop away, revealing the darker nature of capitalism that always lurks just below the surface.

Part of the reason I hate take-overs is because I've been on the other side of the coin. I've been present when asked to "dress up a bit" to meet my new masters. I've been looked at coldly by strangers, knowing that they are weighing my every move. I hear their silent thoughts:

> ***Am I meat—worth keeping—or am I the fat that is to be indiscriminately hacked away in the name of "cost reductions"?***

Lay-offs

Lay-offs are, in theory, much better than getting fired and marginally better than take-overs. In many cases, a lay-off is just that: they are letting you go for now because they no longer have work for you *at this time*. Some businesses periodically go through cycles of booms and busts, inevitably leading to lay-offs. When the work comes back, so do the jobs.

In other cases, however, getting laid off or getting fired amount to the same thing. Frequently, companies tell you that you are being "laid off", but have no intention of rehiring you in the future. Legally and emotionally, it can be easier for both sides that way. Another benefit is that people who are laid off are eligible for federal unemployment benefits, while people who are let go for incompetence, or who quit, are not.

Another possible bonus to the lay-off scenario is the potential willingness on the part of the employer to offer severance pay. This can be as much as one week for every year served. This option is more often possible in a take-over situation, as the company will have money for this sort of thing. If they are just chopping departments to save cash, they are unlikely to be so generous.

When it's Thanksgiving and you're the Turkey

For one reason or another, many of us reach a point in our careers at which we fear for our jobs. Here are a list of long range and short-range steps to take in your own defense:

1. Be Ready For A Surprise Review Meeting At All Times.

Often when lay-offs are coming, management will perform an "employee-review" prior to the grim event. People with lame answers will be handled like lame horses, so you must appear fit. To prepare, be ready with a list of specific and recent accomplishments. Always have an instant answer to the question: "What have you done for us lately?"

2. Don't Look Sick, Tired, Or Otherwise Incapacitated.

Even if you are, don't talk about it. If you are going to the doctor a lot, shrug your shoulders and say: "It's no big deal. I'm fine."

One day Bill, a co-worker of mine, was carrying a heavy computer up the stairs to his office. He strained his back in the process and had to sit down on the steps. It was sometime before he could get up again, as his back was spasming. He joked with a group of us who gathered around that maybe he could get workman's compensation for this. We all laughed and helped him up and carried the computer to his office for him.

A week later he was laid off. There was no clear reason given, but I learned later through the grapevine that his joke had cost him his job. The remark had so rattled the management of our small company that they referred to him as: "That workman's comp. guy." I pointed out repeatedly that he had never even filed for, nor planned to file for, workman's compensation. Eventually, I was able to get his job back for him.

As he told me later: "Now, when my back hurts, I just turn my grimace into a smile."

Gone too, are the days when pregnant women proudly announced their status to a smiling office staff. This is still fine if your job is safe, but it's impossible for employers who are strapped for cash to see your condition as an upcoming "blessed event". Instead, they see higher insurance premiums, a less effective employee and guaranteed frequent absences from work in the near future. A good friend of mine learned this the hard way, getting axed from her new construction design job just a few days before she was eligible for medical insurance.

It's cold-hearted to winnow out the infirm, and in many cases there are laws against it, but it can be impossible to prove in court. Most employers know the laws better than you do, and will leave you no legal recourse.

Unless you are willing to fight about it in court, the best thing you can do is keep quiet, cheerful and healthy—no matter what.

3. Never Openly Attack Your Immediate Superior.

Don't hide their mistakes, but don't point them out, either. If you have something negative to tell your boss, do it privately.

4. Maintain Open Lines Of Communication.

Talk with as many people around the company as possible. Spend ten to twenty minutes a day making friends. Find ones that can help you and who will spill their guts about what is happening elsewhere in the company. This doesn't mean you are a gossip. Don't give away too much information. You should be someone who seeks out the gossips and listens.

5. Maintain Your Contacts On The Outside As Well.

Lunch is made for this purpose. Friends inside the company will keep you in. Friends on the outside will get you out. When your job is on the line, that is when you need your friends most.

6. Don't Just Give Up On The Place And Decide You Don't Care.

You should decide that this is just a job, that it doesn't run your life, but you do care enough to fight for it. Try not to stress out about it, but rather take solace in the thoughtful moves you've made to protect yourself.

7. Build Up A War Chest And Keep It In A Separate Bank Account.

Two months salary is a good level. This isn't part of your investment portfolio; this is liquid cash, probably in a money market account, that will keep the bank from foreclosing on your house and repoing your car someday.

8. If You Are Reasonably Sure That You Are Doomed, Start Looking For A New Position.

Do it discreetly. If you want, you might flash a job offer from someone else at them when you are going down. Sometimes, they may realize that you are more valuable than they thought. At least you will feel better about getting the ax.

9. If You And Your Spouse Work At The Same Company, Try To Get One Of You Out Of It.

It isn't a good idea to work for the same place anyway and many companies have rules against married couples working together, but it is common nonetheless. When the company is stressed for any reason, you can't risk losing both your jobs at the same time. This means that the one who is under the most pressure, or the one who can escape the most easily, should consider leaving.

10. I Am Among The Last To Turn To Legal Action.

I don't believe that our time is best spent wrangling in a courtroom for some years hoping to get a few dollars at the end (most of which, of course, are bound to go to the lawyers). I believe that in most cases, even if your termination seemed unfair, you will do better to go with the recommendation of your old management than a lawsuit. It's better to spend your time and energy looking for something new than squabbling over what was.

However, if you feel you are going to lose your job due to some unfair practice, the time to prepare to defend yourself is now. If there is favoritism or harassment involved, document it. Keep a journal of events such as phone calls, meetings and hallway conversations. Better yet, keep copies of memos that prove you have been treated unfairly. Above all, if you are terminated, don't sign anything that says you waive your legal rights. Not even if they threaten to hold onto your last paycheck. Most states have good laws against this sort of thing.

The Exit Interview

This is a grim, post-mortem process in which you are often informed of your demise and immediately asked to sign a pile of legal documents while you are still in shock. My recommendation to you is to avoid signing anything other than the back of your last paycheck as you deposit it. At least, be careful to read what you are signing. Ask to take it home and bring it back signed the next day. This will give you a chance to think.

Worse, you will often be asked a list of questions about your experiences with the company. Believe it or not, they really do this. Try not to be too negative, as you've got nothing to gain from it at that point.

The biggest bargaining chip you have now is your cooperation and your signature. You should request immediate letters of recommendation from the company before you sign anything. In most cases, you will be able to get them.

Chapter Twenty-One
Resigning, Going Broke and Getting Fired

"What the world really needs is more love and less paperwork."

--- Pearl Bailey

Okay, let's say you can't avoid it. You are leaving the company, or it is leaving you. Let us count the ways:

Resigning

Sometimes there are volatile characters in a group that feel the need to resign periodically. They do it emotionally, or sometimes even as a ploy. I've known several of these. They are particularly common among technical middle managers. About every six months or so, usually in a heat of passion after some kind of management argument, they will stomp out to compose yet another windy letter of resignation.

This is among the worst moves that a technical manager can make, by the way. Instead of "shaking up" their co-workers so they will listen to reason, it often does the opposite. Of course, they will be concerned about your status—the first time. But as soon as you allow yourself to be consoled or simply change your mind, they will think even less of your ideas than they did before. People don't like quitters, but they hate histrionics. Older folks might recall the lesson of Ross Perot and the 1992 presidential election for instant proof of this.

If you resign, you must do it with finality. That means that it is for real, and that you're ready to take the consequences, financial and otherwise. Resignation letters should be short and sweet to the point of rudeness. Don't tell them why you're quitting, no matter how much fun it is. After you leave, the main thing your old company can do for you is help you get your next job. Complaints, especially written ones, will not help you achieve this goal.

At that point, you and the company no longer owe each other anything officially, other than payment for work done and the return of borrowed properties. Two weeks notice is customary, and not a bad idea. Most new jobs can wait two weeks for you. Your new employer will probably like and respect the idea that you have some loyalty to your previous employer. More than two weeks is almost always too much.

Going Broke

It was a cool, crisp Monday morning in Reston, Virginia for Ed, and he might have enjoyed it if he hadn't been late for work. In his haste to beat his boss into the office, he spilled a dollop of his fast-food coffee on his pants. Although it pained him, he thanked the all-American style of navy blue suits -- the stain was sure to be invisible.

He turned into the parking lot and pulled up in front of his building. There was a crowd at the door, but he hardly noticed them in his rush to get to his office. Gulping down the last cool swallow of coffee, he tossed the paper cup into the can and hiked up the steps to the door.

"Hi Ed," muttered the group at the door. He saw the odd looks on their faces, but still it didn't really register. Then he focused on the door as grabbed the door handle.

It didn't open because there was a chain on it. The chain jingled musically as he tugged at it and the heavy padlock clanked a deeper note.

"It's locked, Ed," explained a sadly amused co-worker behind him.

"What's going on?" demanded Ed.

> *"We're broke. The company has filed chapter eleven. They've gone bankrupt."*
>
> *Ed looked around at the others in alarm. "But what about my stuff?" he asked. "I've got a leather jacket in there..."*
>
> *The others shook their heads. Some appeared angry, the rest were shocked and despondent. "There's no one to let us in. Everything inside has been seized to pay for debts."*

And there Ed was left that fine morning. He tells me he has yet to get back his jacket, because he had left it in someone else's office. He did recover some of his personal photos and so forth.

Ed's case was somewhat unusual, but sudden bankruptcy does occur, especially with smaller, younger companies. The trick here is to watch for signs of the company's demise, and to get out before it goes down completely.

If you work for a dying company all the way to the end, you've done nothing for your resume. Often, people on the outside don't know how bad things are. The time to leave is when you can see what is happening, but those who are on the outside (and who might hire you) can't.

Riding a ship all the way down to bankruptcy is probably worse than being laid off or quitting. Why?

Because what good is a recommendation from a company that doesn't exist anymore? Even if you are able to get that recommendation, how can people call the company and check up on your references if the company doesn't exist? It can be difficult to prove what you did and what you know in this situation.

Your reputation is tied to the success of the organizations that you were previously associated with. If they do well, you will be seen as a success. If they flop, you will share part of the blame, regardless of your hand in matters one way or the other.

Because of this, it's best to get out before the house burns to the ground. Switch jobs before your new employers hear about the coming doom and you will be able to do much better.

Getting Fired

It was a gray Thursday morning in California, a few days before Christmas. The moment I arrived at my office, I saw the blinking red light on my phone. Before I could even check my voicemail, the phone rang.

It was the president of the company. He sounded tired and beaten. Right away, I knew it was bad news. He told me he was going to fire my good friend Keith today.

Why was he being let go? The reasons don't matter now, and they didn't seem to matter then, either. I will say that part of it had to do with "the college degree excuse" in that Keith was less valued as an employee than he should have been due to his lack of a degree. In any case, the Boss gave me no time to argue about it.

*He hung up. Suddenly, what had looked like a normal holiday-season cruising-day had turned grim. This time it wasn't me, but my friend who was under the gun. And Keith was a **real** friend, not just an acquaintance. The night before Keith and I had gone to the movies to watch an action-thriller. It had been a "boys night out" and now, the very next morning, this bomb was being dropped on my lap. Soon, the bomb was going to land on Keith as well.*

I sat in my office, eyeing the phone for perhaps thirty seconds while the shock wore off and my brain started to churn. I felt I had to personally warn Keith. I called his extension, and to my relief he picked up. I told him that I had heard his job was in trouble, and to prepare to defend himself anyway he could. Perhaps he could talk his way out of it. The news came as a total surprise to him, and I wished him well...

In the end there was no getting out of it for Keith, or for another of our employees that day. It didn't go well, as there were personality conflicts and quite a bit of shouting. There were only twelve of us working in the local office, so two less made quite a hole. I think the grimmest moment came when our personnel manager quietly removed two of the "luck of the draw" gifts from beneath our miniature, desktop Christmas tree.

What Next?

Getting fired is akin to dying. If you work with an organization for years and enjoy yourself, your job becomes a very significant part of your life. Just think about it: we spend most of our productive waking hours every year at work. The people we work with can be as important to us as our families. As far as stress-levels are concerned, studies show that getting fired from a serious job is right up there with divorces and car accidents.

The good news is that it often isn't a devastating event for long. If you've properly prepared for this possibility and you keep your wits about you it can turn into a positive thing. Sometimes it takes getting axed for people to wake up and realize that they weren't enjoying themselves at that job anyway, which probably helped cause their termination. I don't know how many times I've been told by someone six months later: "Getting fired was the best thing that ever happened to me."

The first thing to do when you leave a company, for any reason, is to pamper yourself for a day or two. Tell a few friends, cry on a few shoulders, eat chocolate and drink beer (or whatever your favorite combination is). Physical activity is very good for the soul at times like these. Try to get outside and tell yourself you're better off in the open air than working in that stuffy old office anyway.

After a few days, however, it's time to get down to business. Apply for unemployment immediately. You've been paying for it for some time, now it is there for you. The checks take a while to come, so don't wait around to sign up.

Next, get out the Rolodex and call everyone you can think of that might hire you, or get you a lead on a job. Frequently in the technical field people will find themselves back to work within a few days.

It is best to do this with an authoritative air, as if you are just considering your options, and haven't actually left the company yet. For some reason, when you are laid-off, fired, whatever, people tend to begin treating you as if you have some kind of infectious disease and don't have the same flame to hire you. Being a bit vague as to your status is a good idea.

Whatever happens, remember that it isn't the end of the world. All it means is that you are out on the open job market again, along with 1 in 20 other Americans at any given time. You are in the selling phase again, and it is time to find a new buyer. Being out of work is not anything unnatural or uncommon. It's just part of the cycle of capitalism. It happens every day to people just like you.

The only difference is that now it's your turn.

Made in the USA
Las Vegas, NV
16 December 2021